# The Secret Asset Shield

Wayne Richardson

Published by Wayne Richardson, 2022.

THE SECRET ASSET SHIELD

First edition. April 14, 2022.



ISBN: 979-8201320744

Written by Wayne Richardson.

# Table of Contents

# Dedication

This book is dedicated to the two most important women in my life. First to my mother, Mary Lou Richardson, who for 83 years has given me unconditional love and has been the best mother a son could ever have. I will always and forever love you Mom, and

thank you for everything you have done for me.

And second, to my wonderful daughter, Kathryn Porter, who gave me the inspiration to get out of bed each morning and strive a little harder on becoming the best Dad I could

be and giving me the gift of my two precious grandchildren, Levi, and Annie Lou, of whom I am so immensely proud.

# Chapter 1 Introduction

Congratulations! If you are reading this book, you are a fortunate person. If you own any real estate, and are considering investing in it, you belong in a very exclusive group.

According to the IRS, less than 8% of all Americans who file a tax return, invest in income producing real estate. Hopefully, after reading this, you will see the value to protect your personal residence and real estate investments, with this easy-to-use but powerful asset protection information.

My intentions for this book are to give the reader an in-depth understanding on the use of asset protection entities, and how to use them to avoid frivolous lawsuits. A sizable percentage of real investors may have heard of these entities, but do not have the knowledge on how to use them to protect their assets to the fullest.

In today's litigious world, it is important to understand that the fundamental purpose of asset protection is to shield assets from unforeseen attacks by dubious creditors or plaintiffs. If you are sued, and as a result you lose your home, car, bank accounts, and brokerage accounts, wouldn't you have wished you had done some planning on keeping your assets safe?

Asset protection means minimizing liabilities. It is the legal process of titling both personal and business assets into entities. You are putting your assets beyond the reach of potential creditors and liabilities, while at the same time enjoying the benefits of those assets. The three entities that we use in asset protection for real estate, is the land trust, limited liability company, and family limited partnership. They all separate ownership, but still give you full control of the asset.

A lawsuit claim can be deleterious to a bright financial future. It really does not matter what the circumstances are, no matter who is at fault, a lawsuit will be expensive in time, money, and stress.

You either settle out of court, or fight it, never knowing how it will end up. You are always susceptible to a plaintiff's lawsuit, if you own low-hanging fruit, which are assets that's in your personal name.

A pending lawsuit can come from other businesses, employees, business partners, past marriages, relatives and especially tenants living in your real estate investments.

With a little knowledge of how to search, and access to an internet, anyone can discover all your personal information. This includes your real estate, cars, boats, bank and investment accounts.

It is unfortunate that we live in such a sue-happy society where we are never more than one mistake away from putting a lifetime of work at risk. Given the volatility of running any business, and especially operating real estate, people will occasionally make mistakes that can potentially threaten their long-term financial future, and many pay that price each day. If your insurance policy is not large enough to cover a judgment claim, it will be your assets that are at risk in the event of a lawsuit.

This could mean, what you have, could become what they have, in the event of a lawsuit. In simple terms, asset protection means separating ownership from assets. Through various proactive steps that need to be taken ahead of time, you can build a shield around your assets. The hope is to discourage attempts of being sued in the first place, by having your assets invisible to the public eye, and judgment proof.

Once a case goes to court, you have little to no control over the outcome, and can only wonder if the judge is going to take everything that you have worked hard for. Asset protection is necessary in order to give yourself the peace of mind you deserve, when you lay your head down each night to sleep.

Protecting your assets means that you preserve them for both your personal use, and for the use of family in later generations. By taking a few of these asset protection steps, you can change the form of ownership of your assets and make it difficult for creditors to reach. These structures will create some separation between you and your assets, that limits your amount of liability in the event of a lawsuit.

There is never a magic wand that will give you absolute protection over every asset that you own. But you want to use the best strategies possible to protect as many assets as you can. It is important to remember that asset protection steps have to be established before any lawsuit claim is filed against you.

This is the reason this is important in establishing asset protection in advance. Your options are extremely limited, once a lawsuit has been filed. Any transfer of property after a lawsuit, could be construed as a fraudulent transfer by the courts, and be undone, and you lose the asset to the judgment. You may think that your wealth is safe, and you do not need asset protection. But my friend, that is living in a delusional world.

For every 60 minutes you spend making money, spend 60 seconds thinking about how you can protect it.

Just think of all the contingence attorneys that are working each day. They make their living on taking money away from someone. It is an insurance company that usually pays that claim. If the awarded judgment is larger than the policy amount, or for some reason the insurance does not cover the liability, you are responsible for the balance. Your assets will be sized and liquidated to pay the judgment.

This is the cold hard facts that happens when a lawsuit is awarded against you. Preparation to protect your assets is as important as the effort to build those assets. Your hard-earned assets can be taken a lot quicker than they are attained by a unforeseen lawsuit that happens to have your name as a defendant.

# CHAPTER 2 Unfortunate Events

———

Just look at the recent deadly event of Alec Baldwin's tragic mistake on 10/ 21/ 2021. When thinking a prop gun had blanks in it, he fired it when practicing a scene, and accidently killed Halynn Hutchinson on the movie set. Since the shooting, Baldwin has been named as a defendant in multiple lawsuits filed over the tragedy, including a wrongful death suit filed by Hutchens husband, Matthew Hutchens.

This will create unimaginable lawsuits for him and many other people that were there doing their assigned jobs.

For example, on 02/04/ 2022, Yahoo News, reported that Cherlyn Schaefer, a medic on the set of Rust, where the Hutchinson incident happened, has filed a negligent lawsuit against the production company, Baldwin, and four crew members working with her on the set because of the tremendous trauma she suffered.

According to her lawsuit, for an undisclosed dollar amount, she cannot return to work again as a medic, because she was so traumatized by Hutchinson's death. She incurred "lost earnings, earning health capacity expenses, emotional trauma and suffering, and loss of enjoyment of life. It added that she is undergoing medical treatment and professional therapy.

Then another tragic event happened at Travis Scott's deadly music concert where ten people were crushed to death on 10/ 5/ 2021. A follow up on the incident, reported by Buzzfeed News, on 02/02/ 2022, stated that over 400 individually filed lawsuits were seeking billions of dollars in damages after the Astroworld tragedy.

Both famous people are subject to losing all of their net worth with the billions of dollars of negligent lawsuits that are filed against them. Not counting the time and stress on a person's health on having to deal with such unexpected tragic events.

**Son's Car Accident**

VERY RECENTLY, I WAS reading this story of an unfortunate event that happened to a father and his son. His 19-year-old son was driving the father's car while on a date, and alcohol was involved.

The son was coming from a party where he and his friends had been drinking for hours. He had three of them in his father's car and was headed for a local club. A deer came out of nowhere and run at the car. As the son served to miss it, the car ran off the road across a 20-foot ditch and hit a tree head on. Everyone was injured badly, but the boy that was in the front passenger seat sustained head injuries that took his life.

Obviously, the parents sued the father and son, and won a $2.3 million dollar judgment. The fact that the boys had been drinking, and the father's son was legally drunk, didn't help the case any. The insurance covered the legal fees and one million dollars. Of course, that left $1.3 million to collect from the father, since he owned the car.

The parents both owned the car jointly, and therefore, became liable for the judgment along with the son. They lost everything they owned and sadly the father's marriage failed with all the stress caused by the accident and lawsuit.

The problem is that the law treats the property owner as the guarantor of the safety of everyone that comes on the property. If anyone is injured on the property for any reason a frivolous lawsuit can be filed against you. This could be from a disgruntled tenant or anyone regardless of who's fault it is. This is a big legal burden and it's easy to see how lawsuits, frivolous or not, are easily generated in this type of legal system.

When a claim is awarded against you, an attorney can instantly seize all your assets, including your real estate, bank accounts, stock securities, by a few simple documents signed by the judge. Without any access to funds to pay your personal expenses and appeal the case, you are, as they say, dead in the water. Not a place that you want to be financially when you are out of legal options.

I find it interesting that investors never realize they need asset protection, until it's too late. Once, they are served with a lawsuit and found liable, then they cry out, why didn't someone tell me about how to protect my assets before this happened? The most important lesson I have learned about protecting assets is not using secret ninja

techniques, but doing the basic stuff right and using what's pragmatic in the real world.

Most small investors think to themselves, I do not have enough assets for someone to sue me. How would you feel if you lost what few assets you do own? Wealth is relative. It is not only the rich and affluent who need asset protection. If you have any assets, regardless of the present value, they need protection.

It's what you own that determines vulnerability and lawsuits. If you have owned a house for any length of time, you have built up equity to temp a plaintiff's lawsuit. Even the proverbial little old lady that needs help crossing the street, can get into big legal trouble.

For, instance, on one occasion an 85-year-old great grandmother accidentally hit the gas rather than the brake and slammed her Cadillac through a K-Mart storefront, seriously injuring several shoppers.

She was subsequently sued for more than her insurance policy. This was her first lawsuit in eighty-five years, but she will be the first to admit the prospect of losing one's life savings, even at 85, is extremely unpleasant. She later told her attorney, she wished she would have known how to have protected her assets, but it was now too late, and she was going to lose everything that she had worked all her life for.

Unfortunately, this tragedy happens to someone every day. No matter how old you are, there's no age cut off for lawsuits. Because it never happened before, is no predictor of future consequences. What a terrible situation to have accumulated assets by working hard all of your life, and then lose them at the end, by an unexpected lawsuit claim. This is why it's so important that you attain the knowledge to keep your assets safe and something like this from ever happening to you.

# Chapter 3 The American Legal System

The American Bar Association estimates that over 1.3 million active attorneys are registered in the United States in 2020. There are 40 million lawsuits filed each year with an average of nearly 100,000 lawsuits filed each day in the United States. No other country in the world has developed such a complex, expensive, all-pervasive system of courts as the United States. Lawsuits are rampant in this country. Statistics show there is one attorney in this country for every 300 residents, and there are an estimated 150,000 people in law school as we speak.

In addition, to an overabundance of attorneys in the U.S. we are the only country in the world that does not have a "loser pays" legal system. For example, other countries such as England, and Canada have a system where if one loses the lawsuit, they pay his or her own legal fees as well as the opponent. However, in the U.S. this system does not exist. Even if a party to a lawsuit win, he or she is out of his or her legal expenses. What this means is that in the U.S. even if a defendant in a lawsuit win, he or she still loses.

In other countries, one must think twice before bringing a lawsuit to the court system. Is the chance of losing the lawsuit and paying the bills of two attorneys worth the possible outcome?

Any business transaction including purchasing or renting real estate, is subject to a lawsuit. Any business operating in any matter will be sued sooner or later. The country has become a powder keg of litigation explosion. Not if, but when you get sued, everything you have worked hard to create will be at risk. To defend yourself in court can easily reach $50,000 over a frivolous lawsuit, and it is no longer uncommon for awards in negligence cases to exceed one million dollars.

**Lawsuits in Today's Unsafe World**

LET'S LOOK AT THE WORLD today. Every day, more than 100,000 lawsuits are filed in courts across the United States. Most are settled out of court that lead to a stressful bankruptcy or worse. It is estimated that three out of four attorneys practice law in the

U.S. The more money you have, the more you risk being a defendant in a lawsuit. Are we in a litigious society? Frivolous lawsuits have become the new business opportunity. Attorneys don't want to go to court, they want to settle out of court. Most of them file a lawsuit just to settle for a quick payout.

They know most defendants will settle for an amount less the long-drawn-out legal fees it's going to cost to defend yourself. They make their living on the bet that we will settle out of court. They say to the defendant, show us a little money, and we will make all this go away. Ninety five percent of lawsuits are settled out of court.

Attorneys advertise on television to encourage people to pursue their dreams of getting a big settlement by suing. Plaintiffs want to get rich the old-fashioned way, by taking it

from you by whatever means necessary. The "have-nots" dream of getting rich by taking money from the "haves", by a lawsuit claim.

Almost every TV station each day that has a news channel, will have attorney commercials, bragging they can get you a big settlement. Call us now, we are waiting for your call. The attorney points at the client and says, look at the $250,000 settlement we just got Mr. Jones for only a broken wrist. $450,000 for a broken neck. All you have to do is pick up the phone and call us. There's no fee, unless we win. The TV attorney says, "we will be with you all the way", which I think means all the way to the bank to help cash the defendant's claim check.

.

# CHAPTER 4 Today's social media

———

In today's day and age, privacy is becoming a scarce resource. With the rise of social media and search engines, more people are finding their privacy under siege. In a world of Facebook, Tweeting, and many other social platforms, more and more personal information is online.

Famous people are targeted by tenacious paparazzi or unruly protesters, and in the worst cases, they and their families have been personally targeted for kidnapping or worse. All you must do is cut on the news and see how scary the world is. It's more important than ever to make privacy a number one priority in your personal life and investing career.

Owning real estate through a land trust is a time-tested way of protecting your privacy when it comes to your home, your business, and your family. For centuries people have used land trusts for anonymity and privacy of ownership. Confidentiality and privacy of ownership are without a doubt the most important benefits of setting up a land trust.

It's the first step in protecting you financially and personally in the unsafe world we live in today.

Owners of real estate are entitled to just as much privacy as owners of stocks and bonds. Real estate ownership does not need to be, and should not be, a matter of public record. Anyone can see with just a few clicks from a keyboard on what you own, and where you live. In today's world, there are people who will scam you financially, or worse. Look at the elderly people who get scammed each day, that have no defense, except keep their doors locked, and not answer the phone.

The land trust provides an excellent method of acquiring, holding, and disposing of real estate without revealing the owner's true identity. Owners of real property often have a legitimate need to avoid disclosure of their interests. Examples include the acquisition of parcels of land by developers so that sellers do not collude to raise their prices. They often do not want anyone to know where they live, in fear of the safety of their family members.

Court judges need anonymity for protection from unhappy litigants, more than people realize outside of the courthouse. I listened to a tragic story on CNN, where a female judge was killed when she opened her front door, with her young son by her side.

It was reported that, she was killed by a prisoner that she had sentenced a few years before, on a conviction of assault and robbery. He was out on parole, when he shot and killed her.

Unfortunately for the judge, for him to find her address he simply went online to the real estate records. The address of the judge's house was listed on the county's tax records for anyone to search, and thanks to Google, a picture of her house was also online.

Everything was there, to help him get revenge for the time he spent in prison.

Celebrities need protection from mentally unstable enthusiastic fans, like the reported news incident with Lady Gaga having her dogs kidnapped. Another scary incident that happened last year, involves The Real Housewives of Beverly Hills star, Dorit Kemsley. Imagine living in a multi-million mansion in Encino Hills, California and having three men break into your home with your two small children 7 and 5 in bed, in the middle of night.

The intruders held her at gunpoint and reportedly ransacked the house for 20 minutes, stealing the stylish star's jewelry and handbags at an estimated one million dollars.

Fortunately, no one was harmed in the invasion. But you can believe that her social media account had shown her wearing what the robbers were searching for. They knew where she lived and a good idea of the expensive valuables that were in her home.

A news report on TV a few weeks back, made me realize the dangers that Realtors have selling real estate. Fox News reported on a horrible event that happened on December 23, 2021. It was about a lady in Florida, working as a realtor, was shot multiple times and killed while showing a house. The authorities say that her death was related to a former tenant that had been recently evicted. The tenant, Raymond Reese admitted that he killed her, because he thought the agent, Sara Trost owned the house that he recently lived in and had recently been evicted from, for non-payment of rent.

Because he couldn't pay the rent and was evicted, he went in a rage, and wanted revenge. Sara Trost, as Fox News reported, was forty years old, and leaves behind a husband and a young daughter, and was very involved with her Synagogue. She was so loving and caring, Rabbi Biston stated to the news reporters, that she had recently accompanied other congregants on a trip to Israel.

Another example that I read about yesterday, was reported in the New York Times, under "Kidnapping of Bloomberg's Housekeeper", the article poignantly emphasizes the importance of privacy from deranged people.

On 02/ 05/ 2022, an armed man broke into the $45 million dollar property of the former Democratic presidential candidate Michael R. Bloomberg and kidnapped his housekeeper, asking the whereabouts of Mr. Bloomberg's two adult daughters, the authorities said. Fortunately, his daughter was not there at the time.

The man, Joseph Beecher, 48, faces charges of kidnapping and breaking and entering, after he was accused of ramming his pickup truck through the main gate of the Westland's Ranch in Rio Blanco County, Colorado on Mr. Bloomberg's 4,600-acre ranch. He forced the housekeeper at gunpoint, to drive them in her truck 230 miles to the Denver area, and later to a town near the southern border of Wyoming, before the authorities tracked them both to a motel there. She was forced that night to sleep in the same bed with him with her head on his chest.

Mr. Beecher and the housekeeper was tracked to the hotel, and he was arrested by the swat team, the authorities said, and an AR-15-style rifle and several magazines were located inside with the man. The housekeeper was found unharmed. The two were found after investigators said they used an app on the woman's phone, which was left behind at the ranch to track her iPad to the Wyoming motel.

A spokesman for Mr. Bloomberg, said in a statement that the former mayor was "deeply grateful" to the authorities for "ensuring that no lives were lost and that the victim has been rescued and safely returned to her family.

Privacy is very important in today's society, and a land trust is necessary when it comes to concealing real estate holdings from public record. Privacy today is a necessity for financially and physically safeguarding yourself against unwanted events, and albeit, unwanted people that may have some excuse to cause you harm.

The land trust insulates owners from annoyances of ownership and keeps their wealth from public view. Anyone these days, can be connected to a computer system that does an instance search of property records of a person's house and gives the street address.

Now with help from Google, you can see a satellite image of your house, and the layout of the property, no matter where it's located. But by placing property into a land trust the ownership can be hidden, your address is not listed on the tax records in your name, and you now have anonymity from the public view.

We watch the news every night. Isn't it amazing that it seems like everyone has rights for every action they take, except you? Why is that? It's because society has lost the perception and definition of "right and wrong" on what's important in this world. Now more importantly, you need to protect yourself from a legal system that doesn't recognize correct actions anymore.

These actions are referenced by my wise Mom when we watch the news together, as she reply's as "common sense that people nowadays don't have". My Mom has been around long enough to realize and see the lack of wisdom that is reflected by most people today. And it makes you wonder, what has happened to common sense? Especially, in the people that are supposed to be running this country.

Stealing a quote from the famous founder of Craftmatic Beds that I once worked for as a salesman, and I quote him, ("I've been taught the best, from the best, when they were at their very best").

I have never forgotten that powerful quote that he shared with me that day, on the importance of learning the best information possible, and from the best teachers in their field. And, just as important, what's pragmatic and works best in the real world. As the owner of a company that has advertised on TV for over fifty years, selling adjustable beds, the man's knowledge was very valuable to me and never forgotten.

"The ABCs of Asset Protection" is first to avoid liability if possible. Obviously, the best asset protection strategy is not to get sued. The second is to appear broke, where nobody will want to sue you. And the third is to protect and control the assets you have by using legal entities for maximum protection.

# Chapter 5 Own Nothing, but Control Everything

John D. Rockefeller was famous for saying "Own nothing, but control everything". Mr. Rockefeller was asked by his son, Nelson, on his dying bed, what was the secret to his tremendous business success. He told his son, "Own nothing, but control everything." Basically, what he meant was "what you don't own can't be taken from you".

This is the fundamental rule of asset protection that real estate investors of today forget about. Mr. Rockefeller certainly used land trusts, a legal device which allows you to retain all the benefits of property ownership without exposure to public scrutiny and litigation. Land trusts also kept the government for many years from knowing how large his monopoly was on controlling his business empire.

What would happen if your child were driving your car and engages in an accident, in which they are at fault? Or there is a fire in a rental house you own, and someone is killed because your smoke alarms did not work. This happens every day of the week. But I can hear you thinking these words, "it's not going to happen to me." It is pertinent to realize, just because it hasn't happened before, doesn't mean it's not going to happen in the future. Would your assets be protected if it did? If served with a lawsuit, would you be able to sleep at night, or worry everything is going to be taken?

**First, why is privacy important?**

REAL ESTATE INVESTORS are perceived by the public as people with high income that own assets, and therefore are bigger targets for frivolous lawsuits. The cheapest form of asset protection is personal privacy. One of the simplest forms of privacy is an entity called a land trust.

To own real estate requires a deed recorded at the county recorder's office. This recording is public information. Many investors don't want their names showing up that they own many properties. This creates a large target for plaintiff attorneys to go after. If a person incurs liability for any reason, the plaintiff's attorney will first search for assets to determine if the person is able to pay out a judgment.

Once your assets are protected, attorneys working on contingency fees are not going to be so quick to sue, because of the uncertainty of collecting. It is all about the money, and how can they legally take it from you?

If that attorney finds assets in your name, you can quickly determine that you will be a defendant in a lawsuit. Meaning, the more assets the plaintiff's attorney finds that you own, the larger the lawsuit amount will be. Any amount over what the insurance pays, will be a collection by the sale of your assets. Therefore, McDonalds got sued for a million dollars over a spilled cup of hot coffee. Go figure.

Real estate is again on top of the list as investment strategies. Prices are at an all-time high all in the United States. In most areas they have appreciated substantially in just the last few years. Houses in popular cities are being sold more than the listed price, and faster than the realtors can put a sign in the front yard. In some areas, the price of real estate has doubled within the last year and sells more than the listed price.

Many investors view a portfolio of apartments, office buildings, shopping centers and houses as an attractive alternative strategy in the current low interest investments offered by banks. The chances of being in a lawsuit with all this new buying, selling and owning properties, puts the real estate investor near the top of the liability scale.

What to do? Should you avoid real estate investment because of the high liability potential? Definitely not!

Anyone wishing to put together a complete picture of your assets will first locate and value any properties that you own. Years ago, deeds to property were filed in the recorder's office in the county where the property is located. A comprehensive and accurate search required you to visit the recorder's office at the courthouse.

You had to research the "grantee index" for the grantee name that shows all property deeded to that name. You would then have to do this for each county you searched in. It was a time-consuming, expensive and inefficient process for researching ownership.

Now anyone with a computer and internet service can do the same thing without leaving their home or office. Your tax records online reveal everything from a picture of your home, what you paid for it, the value now, and when you purchased it.

Your properties are now at risk, in the event of a lawsuit. There are companies that attorneys use that will provide all your financial information, such as your bank accounts, brokage accounts, real estate, and any asset you have ever owned in the past.

You cannot hide assets that are titled in your name. In today's information world, they will be found. It's amazing how much information can be attained about someone by these information seeking companies with the push of a few keys on the computer.

I was recently invited to spend two hours on a zoom call, with a "Pre-Trial Focus Group" for a trial attorney's upcoming trial. I was to listen and give my opinion about the attorney's trial case that involved a young lady that had lost her eyesight. They wanted the opinions of the six of us participating, on how we thought the case would turn out when it went to court in a few coming weeks.

The young lady had slipped and fell getting out of bed, hit her head, and was having problems with her vision. On the morning it happened, she called 911 and the rescue squad carried her to the hospital, and she was released after a few hours. The hospital doctor examined her, and she was told by the doctor, that her partial loss of eyesight would return after some time and rest.

The young lady's eyesight had not improved after a few days, so she visited an ophthalmologist to get his medical opinion. She was told by him, it would be temporary loss of vision, and her eyesight would return to normal. She was given some medication and was scheduled to return in two weeks. In that time period she went completely blind, and is now suing the ophthalmologist, the hospital, and the hospital doctor who first examined her for negligence malpractice.

During the Focus Group we were asked how much money do you think she deserves if she wins the lawsuit? It was suggested by some in the group that the lawsuit award should be at least one million dollars. The plaintiff's attorney is suing everyone that was involved and hoping to win a big settlement.

The point is, if you are involved in an incident, your fault or not, you will be named as a defendant in the litigation. This means an expensive attorney bill will be the least of your problems. It is not going to be pleasant, one way or another, even if you are not found liable in the lawsuit.

A defense attorney always gets his fees in a trial, win, or lose. Then factor in time, stress, and aggravation on top of the money it's going to cost you. I will gamble that the golden years for some people will never be too golden and come to fruition, because an unexpected lawsuit took their assets, and caused serious health and relationship problems is their lives.

After a judgment is awarded to the plaintiff, location of the debtor's assets become the focus of the plaintiff's attorney. The debtor's exam may be presented by written questions or by oral examination. The debtor will have to list and describe all of his real estate holdings, and provide all banking records, including brokerage accounts, and all assets of value.

You will also be asked whether you have made any transfers of any property by gift prior to or during the lawsuit. All these questions are asked under oath, and the failure to provide true and complete answers is a felony and can result in prison time if not answered truthfully. (Just ask Martha Stewart how she knows:)

When a judgment has been entered, the court issues a "writ of execution," which is essentially an authorization for the collection action. The judgment creditor gives the writ of execution to the sheriff with instructions describing the property and all assets of yours to be seized.

The sheriff is authorized to take possession of your property and assets. Real property seized in this matter may then be sold at public auction. Your bank accounts and brokerage accounts can also be seized in this matter, and any party that owes you money is notified that they must make payment directly to the sheriff's office.

The collection procedure for your real estate begins with the filing of a summary of the judgment called "abstract of judgment", filed in each county you own real estate. The abstract of judgment creates a lien on the property automatically without having to designate the address of the property. The lien will also attach to any real estate purchased in the future that's titled in your personal name.

Once this abstract of judgment has been filed, your property cannot be sold or refinanced without satisfying the judgment. Trying to transfer the property to a third party also will not work. The judgment lien remains attached to the property until the judgment is satisfied or expires. In most states, this is ten years and can be renewed for another ten years.

When an attorney files a lawsuit against you, he is exploiting the deepest fears of human nature. He knows that the outcome of the case will be uncertain regardless of the merit of the case. He knows that if you have reachable and collectible assets, the risk of loss will cause you extreme worry and stress. He has you in a situation of panic and fear of the unknown that could become very expensive. He knows exactly how afraid you are, and he enjoys every minute of the intimidation.

# CHAPTER 6 Fear of the Unknown

———

Finally, he knows that if you choose to fight the case, your time and your privacy will be violated, and your resources will be depleted or exhausted by needless legal fees and costs. It's so much more appealing and logical just to settle quickly out of court. If you have available and reachable assets such as real estate, which can be uncovered by a simple search, then the attorneys hold the leverage, and know that most defendants will settle the case out of court.

Nowadays because of the number of attorneys and lawsuits filed each day, attorneys are looking for new deep pockets to go after for easy low hanging fruit. The new "deep pockets" are those that have saved up some money for retirement, equity in real estate investments, and just as importantly, have assets in their personal name.

Real estate investors are particularly vulnerable for two reasons. The first is that the real estate ownership is shown in the public records for anyone to find. The second is that any judgment against you immediately becomes a lien against all your other real estate assets, if recorded in the county where the property is located.

This judgment will lien your properties until you either pay it off or win a later appeal. If a potential defendant is an individual or a small company, the plaintiff's attorney is going to do substantial investigations before he commits his time and resources in a case that pays no dividends.

You must assume then, that the attorney interested in suing you will perform a thorough financial investigation of your background, assets, and income. All your assets will be susceptible to a lawsuit. Any effort to conceal them now, could be undone by a judge.

Therefore, asset protection needs to be done in advance to avoid any fraudulent transfer accusations.

# CHAPTER 7 You Have Been Served

Now let us look at what happens when a regular apartment building owner named Mr. Smith gets sued. He purchased his building thirty years ago in his personal name, and it generates a good monthly income for him. He has never thought about placing the property into an entity for asset protection. The property has given him no trouble through the thirty years he has owned it.

He gets up one morning and there is a knock on his door. He is being severed with a lawsuit from a (contingent fee attorney). The lawsuit states that he, "Mr. Smith" is being sued because one of his tenants in his 10-unit apartment building was broken into, robbed, and beaten by an assailant. The lawsuit claims that there were inadequate locks on his tenant's door to prevent the break in from occurring.

Because of this robbery, the negligence claim against Mr. Smith includes pain and suffering, medical bills, legal fees, loss of income, private property replacement, and perhaps long-term disability payments. The ultimate amount of the damage award cannot be predicted with any level of confidence. Mr. Smith's insurance policy has denied the claim because of negligence of not replacing the original locks with additional deadbolts and view holes.

Now if Mr. Smith loses the trial, the case will be moved on to the collection stage of the lawsuit. Let us assume that Mr. Smith lost the case and there's been a judgment awarded against Mr. Smith for $600,000, and his insurance policy finally agreed to pay a very small portion of it. He could appeal the judgment to a higher court but would be required to post a security bond equal to the amount of the judgment.

To appeal, Mr. Smith will have to obtain the appeal bond through a licensed bonding company that would require him to post security equal to his $600,000 bond. That usually means that the property posted would have to have a much greater value, in case it had to be sold to net the bondsman $600,000.

Then you must add in the bondsman's fee which is usually 10% of the bond which adds another $60,000 to the cost. This is for the privilege of filing the appeal, then to make matters worse, Mr. Smith will have to pay for trial transcripts and retain an appellate attorney who will charge him another $75,000 or more.

During the time that the case is on appeal, the judgment creditor would not be permitted to take any steps to collect on the judgment. After the appeals are exhausted, the judgment creditor will then begin the collection process.

The example above shows that appeals are fine for large corporations that have the financial ability to pay for them, but for the average person the right to appeal is an illusory consolation, because of the tremendous expense of appealing.

Don't make the mistake that Mr. Smith made and lose everything because you didn't

take the time to get that property out of your name. It is worth the small effort it takes to set up a land trust in conjunction with an LLC, to protect your assets with privacy and asset protection. Your future self will thank you for it, especially when a lawsuit does not have your personal name as the defendant.

Liability Insurance is important because it is the first thing that is looked upon in a claim.

Having insurance is so important in asset protection. It really should be called the first rung on the ladder of asset protection. A judge can easily disregard an entity in court, if there is no liability insurance for that entity, because you treated the business as your alter ego, and not a real business. Liability insurance often works well with creditors in post-judgment circumstances.

Oftentimes, once a creditor realizes how difficult it will be to reach your assets. He will just take the insurance policy proceeds and settle out of court for an easy payday.

Liability insurance is thus a diversionary tool. Having at least moderate liability insurance is an essential component of a comprehensive asset protection plan.

# CHAPTER 8 My First Real Estate Mentor

I first learned about land trusts, and their benefits in Orlando Florida, while attending a real estate seminar held by Mark O. Haroldsen in the late 1980s. He was a big apartment investor, but started out with buying and rehabbing run-down houses, that he called dirt-bag homes. At that time, he had become very well known for writing the popular real estate investing book ("How to Wake Up the Financial Genius in You.")

He was one of the first real estate investors that held annual investing seminars throughout the country. He also put out a monthly real estate investing magazine called "The Financial Freedom Report", which was the catalyst for me and many others to start investing in real estate. Not like today's available information that you can find on YouTube and real estate podcasts.

At this early stage of my investing career, my wife and I attended one of his events in Orlando, Florida. The most pertinent lesson that I learned from attending the event was how easy it is to lose your assets from a lawsuit. I learned how the land trust could conceal your assets and keep them off public record.

Ever since that early seminar, I have been using land trusts in conjunction with other entities to protect my properties. I would like to personally thank Mr. Haroldsen, for all the great information provided on his real estate investing seminars, and for giving me the courage to take that first step so many years ago. Thank you, Mark.

Hopefully my investing days are not over yet, and I'm very motivated to get going again after this Covid 19 shut down. I am renewed again, and now have two beautiful grandchildren to motivate me to be able to help them some day.

I was totally amazed when I first learned how a land trust worked to hide real estate. I was reminded that the trust worked like a cloaking device that was featured on one of my favorite TV shows I watched as a young boy, "Star Trek".

The original TV series many years later, was turned into the mega blockbuster movies that become such popular hits. I remember watching some of the early TV episodes, when Captain James T. Kirk was fighting his alien nemesis, the Klingons. The alien Klingons had this secret cloaking device that made their spaceship disappear and shielded it from detection. The Klingons had developed the ultimate clandestine fighting system.

This secret device made their Klingon Bird-of-Prey spaceship vessel impossible to see and fire upon. This was the secret weapon that gave the Klingon's vessel a supreme advantage over Captain Kirk's spaceship USS Enterprise.

Amazingly, this is exactly what the land trust does for real estate. It is a cloaking device that conceals your real estate interest. It gives you anonymity by concealing your real estate, but still giving you full control of the property with a simple trust agreement and a nominee trustee.

**First Benefit of my Land Trust**

THE LAND TRUST WORKS in protecting you from all creditors including IRS liens. This was one of my first lessons on learning the power of a simple land trust over Uncle Sam, otherwise known as the Internal Revenue Service.

One year, the IRS changed the tax structure with their "flat minimum tax" which was based on paying a flat tax on gross income. I ended up with a substantial IRS tax bill that I received in the mail from the IRS. They were calling me in for the dreaded tax audit. During my office audit, the IRS agent showed me what they had estimated I owned for back taxes and penalties.

It was substantial, and due now. I explained that at the time, I could not pay that amount and I also did not think it was fair to me. Because I was not allowed to use all my expenses to reduce the bill and had to pay their flat tax. After, a few back and forths, the IRS agent threatened to place a tax lien on my home if the tax bill was not paid within a brief period of time. If not eventually paid, the IRS explained to me that they could foreclose on my home. But, when the IRS agent pulled up my home address on the tax records, he realized that my home was in a trust.

He asked me in an incredulous voice, "Your house is in a trust?" I said, yes sir it is. And guess what? That was the last time the IRS agent said anything about placing a lien on my home. He kept looking at the tax record like he could not believe it. This trust had taken his power threat away. He did not know how to deal with a trust.

This stopped the IRS lien dead in its tracks from ever being recorded, because my home was not in my name anymore. We ended our meeting with me negotiating a substantially lower income tax bill. Thanks to my powerful weapon called a land trust.

# CHAPTER 9 What is a Land Trust

———

Ah, this is a great question. A land trust is nothing more than a few pieces of paper designed to hold title to real estate. To create a land trust, you need a "Deed in Trust" (which conveys the property into the trust), and a "Trust Agreement" (a contract between the trustee and beneficiary). Land trusts are a legal way to get your name out of the county courthouse records. Lawsuits are a danger to every real estate owner.

And the best defense against this danger is the famous "Illinois Land Trust."

A land trust is an arrangement whereby one person (the trustee) holds title to property for the benefit of another party (the beneficiary). For example, you have a million- dollars' worth of stock that your stockbroker is investing for you. You receive the stock dividends each month, but the stock is still yours, but the brokerage company holds it in securities for you.

The land trust creates a "Legal Contract" to protect, hold, and manage your real estate for the benefit of yourself and heirs, by a third party called a trustee. A land trust is a private legal contract in which the owner of real estate transfers the title of the property to a trustee. The property owner retains all rights to the property, to build, rent, sell or transfer to heirs, but has the luxury of remaining anonymous. As in any contract, someone must initiate the contract. The contract (trust agreement) must specify the who, what, where, when, why, and give direction (instructions on what to do).

Finally, the trust is for the benefit of someone or something else, called the beneficiary, or beneficiaries. The trustee of a land trust is a nominee, who holds title to the real estate for the benefit of the beneficiary. On their own, a land trust will not protect you from lawsuits, but they can be the first defense of a critical component of an asset protection plan because it creates anonymity. A trust can hide ownership, because an entity such as an LLC, will be on public file in most states and show the name of its owners (members).

Let us observe and examine the land trust's most loved feature, privacy through anonymity. The land trust has one purpose, which is to hold and control real estate rather than have real estate titled in your personal name.

When you use a land trust to buy property no one knows, and it is almost impossible to find out that you are the real owner. Privacy can protect you from lawsuits and give you the freedom to sell your property even if liens and judgments have been filed against your name.

There is no public record in the world that shows who the beneficiaries of a land trust are. The trustee is listed as the owner and only he knows the identity of the beneficiary. Those checking the courthouse records will find no records of the beneficiaries of a land trust.

A real estate land trust is just one of many varieties of trusts. A trust, in legal terms is any arrangement in which one party holds property for another party's benefit. The property owner never gives up control of the assets, cash, stocks, bonds, real estate, but the trustee becomes the owner for legal purposes.

The function of all trusts is to shield the asset owner from certain legal proceedings and tax exposure. A wealthy couple might create a trust to shield some of the assets from estate tax when they die. In the case of real estate land trusts, the trust greatly simplifies the process of passing on the real estate to heirs or new owners. A trust can be either irrevocable, where the arrangement cannot be canceled, or revocable, meaning it can dissolve or be changed at any time.

Trust agreements are "trustee driven", except for the land trust. This means that when the trust is formed, the trustee has the power and makes the decisions about with the trust's assets. His duty is to do what is best for the trust. He has full control of what happens in the trust. The beneficiary or beneficiaries have no say in the trust arrangements.

This is (**NOT**) the case with a land trust. Land trusts are "beneficiary driven" meaning that the **beneficiary** of the trust makes all the decisions about the trust and directs the trustee to act according to the wishes of the beneficiary. In the land trust agreement, the control is deemed to the beneficiary. Therefore, a trustee cannot do anything, until the **"written direction to trustee is given by the beneficiary"** which have full control over the land trust.

The beneficiary controls the land trust, not the trustee. The trustee is a nominee, who is directed by the beneficiary and has no control except what is directed to him or her by the beneficiary. So, you have full control of what goes on with the property and all control. Therefore, a land trust is unique and gives you full control of your property and allows you to make all decisions.

Remember a regular trust agreement drawn up by an institution will place the control of your property to a trustee, and not you. The institution can now charge you for fees associated with the trust.

A land trust is designed for one thing, which is to hold land, and control almost anything to do with real estate, including mortgages, leases, and notes. This land trust is a special trust that is only used for real estate transactions and holds no other assets.

Another unique feature of a land trust is that the trustee is considered to hold both legal and equitable title to the real estate. **Because of this, the beneficiary's interest in the real estate is transformed into personal property.**

(Legal title means the person who is listed as the owner of the property in the official records of ownership), and (equitable title means the person who is really entitled to the property). This is what makes the land trust so special, and a unique tool for real estate asset protection.

This concept is difficult for people to understand because the beneficiary still has the right to possession, rents, profits, management and the like as if he still owned the property. The owner would still have equitable title.

**So, what does an owner of a land trust hold, if he does not have legal or equitable title? He holds an interest in the trust that's called a beneficial interest. The land trust's beneficial interest is now legally considered personal property, instead of real property. The land trust holds title to the property by a trustee.**

**Avoiding Litigation**

A LAND TRUST IS SO important for investors in creating anonymity. It gets the investor's name off the title. Consider this, you, the investor, have ten pieces of property, and you have a slip and fall on one of them. A plaintiff's attorney searches your name on record and sees you own nine other pieces of property.

What are the chances that you are going to have a frivolous lawsuit on your hands? Very high indeed. Hey, this is a wealthy person who has money and assets, thinks the plaintiff's attorney. I know he will settle quickly out of court for a quick payday for me. All I will need to do, is scared him with my big bad lawsuit.

Now, turning that same scenario on the other side, the property is owned by a trust that owns one property. Your chances of getting sued just dropped precipitously. Savvy real estate owners know it is extremely important to keep their names from real estate records, because it minimizes risk and keeps your affairs private.

The owners of real estate are easy targets for lawsuits when the property is titled in their personal name. Even a frivolous lawsuit may be worth filing if the defendant has numerous properties that can be tied up in litigation or seized. But if it looks like a person has no assets, it may be difficult for a plaintiff to persuade an attorney to take the case, because the contingency attorney may not get paid even if the suit is won.

Let's look at an example of a real estate land trust. John Smith and his business partners buy an apartment building. They decide that an insurance policy may not be enough protection for them, so they transfer the property into a land trust. They choose a law firm to be the trustee. Since his business partners earn rental income through the apartment building, they are also beneficiaries of the trust.

To help understand the legal benefits of a real estate land trust, let's look at what this transfer of the apartment building deed into the land trust does. The first benefit of a land trust is privacy. Once the title to the apartment building is transferred into a trust, the names of John Smith and his business partners are no longer the legal owner. Their names are off public record as the owners.

Another benefit keeps any personal lawsuit liens against John Smith or one of his partners from ever attaching to the building. Multiple owners of a property aren't punished by legal judgments against only one of them. If John did not have a land trust, it would be damaging to John and the rest of the property owners. With a trust however, the apartment building is shielded from legal actions against one or all the other owners.

Another advantage of remaining anonymous is to avoid litigation. If people think the John Smith is fabulously wealthy, they might dream up frivolous lawsuits against him. But since John's name is off public records, he's less of a potential target.

Another major advantage of a real estate land trust is what attorneys call "ease of conveyance". In other words, it is easy to transfer ownership of the proper heirs without involving lawyers or courts. Usually when someone dies, heirs will have to be approved and their assets appraised through a costly legal process called probate.

Probate can involve back taxes and debts. With a trust, the property owners create a succession and names new beneficiaries upon death. Since the trust itself never dies, no probate is required.

A land trust is very powerful when you look at its ability to create anonymity. This feature alone can stop frivolous lawsuits from happening. Land trusts leave no paper trail which makes it one of the most effective asset protection techniques in existence, for privacy and protection. It truly is a cloaking device that hides your property.

To attain liability protection for them, they can now transfer their beneficial interest in the land trust to an LLC. This would give them liability protection that the land trust does not provide. The land trust is for privacy only. The LLC owning the land trust would provide inside and outside protection for John Smith and his partners.

It's important to realize, there's no reason for anyone to know how many properties you own and where they are located. When your properties are in a land trust, the only recording, is the recorded trustee's name on the deed.

For a land trust to be sued, the trustee must be found, and then summoned to court, and go through a discovery by the plaintiff's attorney, to reveal who is the beneficiary of the trust. This expense by itself, can stop a frivolous lawsuit from ever being filed.

It should be noted, however, that a land trust is not absolute protection against disclosure. It is a barrier that will hide your ownership from view. But as with other types of wealth-minded lawsuits, a court can order you to disclose what you own, if you are involved in litigation, when the claim is big enough.

The land trust will protect people most of the time. It will always give you the time and freedom to deal with your property in the event court actions are taken against you.

Usually, while a lawsuit is pending you do not have to disclose your assets. If your property is in a land trust, you would be free to sell it, even while the case is pending.

**What is Probate?**

ANOTHER VERY IMPORTANT benefit of using a land trust is that the property owned by the land trust does not have to go through probate when you die. It works just like an estate-planning living trust that avoids probate. Probate is a state specific legal process that takes place after someone's death with the purpose of property administering and disposing of their estate. It is a court proceeding where it is decided who gets a deceased person's property.

Probate can be an expensive process with attorney fees and it can take months or even years before the property is released from probate. Probate fees which are paid in order to bring your estate to closure upon your death will take a large chunk of your estate to pay attorneys. Probate is, in summary, the procedural act of proving that a will is valid. Some people believe they can avoid probate if they have a will. This is quite the contrary. A will is the reason that probate exists. There are a lot of attorneys that make their living off of probate fees.

It is these waiting periods that can drastically extend the length of probate at considerable expense and aggravation, because most assets of the state cannot be used and enjoyed by the beneficiaries named in the will. It is easy to see why avoiding probate is such a priority for many estates. A trust will avoid probate, not a will.

If a person owns property in more than one state, a probate must be filed in each state in order to distribute the property at death. This can be avoided by having a land trust hold properties that you own in different states. That is a great benefit if you own investment properties or vacation homes in different parts of the country, that would be subject to probate.

Each step in the probate process contains significant waiting and notice periods. In some states, for example, creditors have 30 days to file a claim with the estate if they received direct notice, 90 days if notice was published but not directly delivered, and 2 years if they did not reasonably receive notice. Many states set the probate fees that an attorney can charge. These fees are often around 8% of the gross worth of the estate.

In most states a land trust can allow property to pass to whomever one chooses without any probate court proceedings. The trust documents usually name contingent beneficiaries and upon the death of the first beneficiary they immediately become the owners of the trust. This avoids both the cost and delay of probate proceedings.

By avoiding probate, a land trust also avoids the complications of a will. If you decide to take someone out of your will in many states, you must prepare a new will or an amendment to the will and formally execute it before two witnesses often in front of a notary public. But to change the beneficiary of your land trust you just put your signature alone on a simple "Amendment to the Trust" form and deliver it to the trustee and it's legal. There is no formality and it's private.

**Avoiding Ancillary Administration Probate**

IF A PERSON OWNS PROPERTY in more than one state, a probate usually must be filed in each state in order to distribute the property at death. Persons who own second homes or investment property in other states can avoid additional probates in those states by owning them in a land trust.

# Chapter 10 Advantages of a Land Trust

Forming a land trust is a necessity for the savvy real estate owner. It helps keep the ownership of the property private and consequently insulates you from litigation. When a land trust is formed with an attorney as the trustee, the attorney legally can't give any information out about the land trust because of attorney-client privilege, unless directed to do so in court.

The beneficiary controls the trust by having the power of written direction to instruct the trustee of any action, and to change trustees at any time if desired, which is spelled out in the land trust agreement. Since the trustee holds title as a fiduciary, they incur no personal liability for merely being on the title. Nor, can the trustee lose the property to his or her personal creditors, because they are simply a nominee trustee for the land trust.

**When To Set Up a Land Trust**

THE BEST TIME TO SET up a land trust is as soon as you purchase your property. The reason for doing this is to keep your name off the property records, and away from creditors. You will need to let the trustee know about your plan on setting up the trust before doing so.

You, as the beneficiary, have ultimate control over the relationship and can revoke the trust at any time. Any real property can be held in a land trust, including a subdivision, development, raw land, condominium building or unit, office complex or an apartment complex.

The land trust also can hold leases, deeds, mortgages, contracts or any dealings with the trust property. The many benefits of a land trust are privacy of ownership, avoidance of probate, protection against judgments and liens, ease of transfer of beneficial interest, use of beneficial interest as collateral, and prevention of property partition.

**Protection From Judgments Against Other Beneficiaries**

A LAND TRUST CAN BE especially beneficial when there are several beneficiaries, and an outside judgment is issued against only one of them. The trust can protect the other beneficiaries against judgments and liens against one beneficiary alone.

A judgment will not constitute a lien on the trust property itself. Rather, it is only a judgment on the percentage of beneficial interest that beneficiary owns in the land trust. The land trust can continue with its normal operations without suffering any legal fallout from the judgment.

Similarly, a land trust protects unaffected beneficiaries against the legal incapacity or personal bankruptcy of one beneficiary. An important benefit of the land trust is that it protects a property against a partition proceeding. Sometimes a beneficiary may wish to liquidate his interest by forcing a division or sale of the property. However, the property in a land trust is owned by the trustee, not the beneficiaries. Thus, without the trustee's explicit approval, no sale or division of a land trust's property can take place. The trustee must have approval, and written direction by all beneficiaries to take any action affecting the trust.

**Real Estate Judgments**

REAL ESTATE JUDGMENTS do not attach to personal property. Let me repeat that again, the beneficial interest of the land trust that you hold, is now personal property. The reason for the conversion of the beneficiary's interest to personal property, is to protect it from judgment liens and other problems associated with owning real estate.

A real estate judgment lien cannot attach to personal property. Like the Klingons spaceship cloaking device on Star Trek, your real estate interest is now gone, but still controlled by you, as the beneficiary of the land trust. The land trust is the only trust that provides this special benefit by changing the legal title vested into the trustee.

Finally, because conveyance of the trust property is made solely by the trustee, a land trust can prevent many of the delays associated with transfers of property held in traditional trusts or other forms of multiple ownership.

For example, delays created by the death, incapacity, bankruptcy, litigation, divorce or no residency of one or more beneficiaries may be avoided by having a land trust hold the property, with instructions in the trust agreement for any successor beneficiaries.

**Keeping Personal Judgments off with the Land Trust**

WHEN REAL ESTATE IS held in a land trust, judgments and liens against the individual beneficiaries do not attach to the land. So, even if judgments are against your personal name in public records, including IRS liens, you can freely sell the property, and direct the trustee of the land trust to wire your funds to any desired account.

# CHAPTER 11 History of Land Trusts

The land trust has been used in our country for over 200 years. The laws behind trusts followed the settlers over from England. Land trusts were first used in the Roman times of King Henry VIII in England. At that time, people used land trusts to hide their ownership of land so they would not have to serve in the military or fulfill other obligations of land ownership. In those days before stocks and bonds, land was the primary form of wealth. The king ruled and wanted to control this wealth. Owners of land had to pay taxes and do military service for the overlord. They were limited to passing it to their oldest sons, they could forfeit it for conduct deemed treason, and they could lose it in payment for their debts.

So, some clever attorneys got together and drew up the agreement that invented the land trust. In which land could be transferred to someone else to hold for the real owner This would circumvent the King's laws so that he could not take the land for these offenses. In 1536 King Henry VIII decided to put an end to the trust business and passed the Statute of Uses. This statute said that where land was placed in a trustee's name for the use of another person, "the use was executed" and the title reverted to the beneficiary. Even though King Henry VIII decided to bypass the use of trusts (to prevent the common man from holding title to property in trust, and avoiding the responsibilities of land ownership), the courts of England upheld the use of the land trust and all rights of the beneficiaries.

In 1545 the English courts made a ruling that the "Statute of Uses" only applied to passive trusts (trusts in which the trustee had no legal duties). It did not apply if the trustee had some minor duties to perform, making the trust active. Since most American law escheats from English Common Law, the use of trusts and the law supporting them was easily blended into American Law that is applied today.

In the late eighteen hundred, Chicago investors figured out that land trusts would be good for buying property to build skyscrapers on. The land trust was formed in the United States by the Chicago Title Company.

A land development company in Illinois wanted to subdivide a large piece of ground that was encumbered by a large mortgage. Since the mortgagee would not release the lots individually until the entire debt was paid off.

Chicago Title became involved with the developer and became the trustee of the entire parcel in a land trust agreement. They guaranteed to the buyers and prospective mortgage companies that free and clear title would eventually be delivered to them.

When enough lots were sold off to pay the mortgage off in its entirety, it worked as planned. It was a successful gamble that paid off handsomely for Chicago Title and the land trust.

Over time the land trust was challenged in court, but the Illinois Supreme Court ruled in 1891 that the land trust was a legal agreement, if the land trust was set up with some minor duty of the trustee. Then the trust would not be considered passive and would be valid. Thus, this worked marvelously, and the land trust was born.

By this court ruling, the land trust in America was born, and is still commonly called the Illinois Land Trust. The land trust has been actively used in Illinois for over a hundred years, and is legal in all states. Some states have specifically legislated laws for land trusts that are addressed in their state.

At the current time, there are only eight states that have laws addressing land trusts. These are the following: Florida, Georgia, Hawaii, Illinois, Indiana, Montana, South Dakota and Virginia. These states acknowledge the land trust through statutes obtained in their state law, and other states allow the use of land trusts via common law.

Common law is based on custom and judicial precedent rather than written state statutes.

The land trust can be used in all states to hold real estate. In some states, it is known simply as a real estate holding trust. It's important to remember that a beneficiary controls a land trust with his beneficial interest, not the trustee. You are always in control of your property with a land trust.

# CHAPTER 12 Walt Disney used Land Trusts

Walt Disney opened his Disneyland resort in Anaheim, California in July 1955. From the moment it opened its doors, it was a soaring success. Disney was looking for a second location to build an even more ambitious theme park that would draw visitors from the length of the populous East Coast where 75% of the population in the United States lived. Disney wanted a park that was close to this population, and he also wanted to have control over a larger land area than he did with Disneyland.

In November 1963, Walt Disney flew over a site close to the sleepy town of Orlando, Florida. It looked promising for a new park. It was a centrally located site and had a good network of roads surrounding it. What solidified the choice for the site was the planned construction of Interstate 4 and its intersection with the Florida Turnpike, on account of McCoy Air Force Base, later Orlando International Airport. In 1965 real estate in this waterlogged stretch of Florida was selling for around $180.00 an acre. Disneyland is the most visited vacation resort in the world, but it might not have been that way if Walt Disney hadn't kept the development a secret in the 1960s.

An announcement that Disney would be building a second resort in Central Florida would have caused land prices to skyrocket as land speculators would have swooped in to get in on the action. Walt Disney Productions used land trusts and holding corporations in different names to acquire 30,500 acres (48 sq miles) of land.

The plan by Disney was to buy up larger tracts of land first followed by smaller tracts, all without anyone knowing the company behind the purchases. In May 1965, these major transactions were recorded a few miles southwest of Orlando in Osceola County. It took Disney six months to close on the first purchase of the land, but they had their start of what would become The Walt Disney World.

The first purchase of land was recorded on May 3, 1965, for 8,380 acres of swamp purchased seven months earlier. After the first purchase was recorded, Florida Ranch Lands Trust, the land trust he was using to make purchases, completed deals with 47 other landowners.

In all, the company purchased 27, 400 acres for more than $5 Million from 51 landowners buying anonymously with land trusts. The average price of the land after the deals were finished was $182.00 an acre. Working strictly in secrecy, real estate agents unaware of their client's identity began making offers to landowners in April 1964, in parts of southwest Orange and northwest Osceola counties.

The agents, without revealing their intentions, were able to negotiate numerous land contracts on large tracts of land for as little as $100.00 an acre.

Eventually, early rumors and speculation about the large land purchases were assumed to be possible developments from major corporations such as NASA in support of nearby Kennedy Space Center, as well as famous investors as Ford, Rockefeller, and Howard Hughes.

The truth was publicly revealed on October 25, 1965. Disney asked Florida Governor Haydon Burns to confirm the story that Disney World was coming. He had no choice because Emily Bavar, an editor from the Sentinel had earlier visited Disney for an interview at Disneyland. She asked Disney if he was behind the recent large land purchases in central Florida. Bavar later described that Disney "looked like I had thrown a bucket of water in his face", before denying the story. Three days later, after gathering more information from various sources, the Sentinel published an article headlined, "We Say: Mystery Industry Is Disney". The secret buyer of all this land had been revealed.

Walt Disney died a little over a year later on December 15, 1966 during the initial planning of the complex. After his death, the company wrestled with the idea of whether to bring the Disney World project to fruition. However, Walt's older brother, Roy, came out of retirement to make sure Walt's biggest dream was realized. So, the building of the park fell to his brother. Disney World opened on October 1, 1971, with a cost of

$400 million. It started with the Magic Kingdom and has grown into multiple attractions over the years.

The total revenue for Disney for 2019 was $26.5 billion. Walt Disney World is the most visited vacation resort in the world, with an average annual attendance of more than 58 million. What about those land prices Disney was worried about in the first place, and why all the secrecy? Following the announcement of Disneyland, land prices skyrocketed in Orlando, where in some cases the land went up to $80,000 an acre. It would have cost Disney almost $2.2 billion just to buy the land for the park at that price.

# CHAPTER 13 How a Land Trust is Formed

A trust is a form of ownership, which is controlled and managed by your designated trustee, that completely separates responsibility and control of trust assets from your benefits of ownership. The IRS separates responsibility and control of trust assets from your benefits of ownership.

The IRS recognizes numerous types of trust used for wealth preservation and legal protection against potential lawsuits, elimination of probate, and elimination of estate taxes. The trustee manages the trust, holds legal title to trust assets, and must exercise and perform all duties assigned to him by the trust. All trust income is taxable to either the trust, beneficiaries of the trust, or corporate entities that own the trust.

Ok, I can see you already rolling your eyes with boredom. Hang with me for a few moments, I promise it will be worth it. These three positions are the same with all trusts. At the end of this chapter, you will be able to impress your friends with your new trust knowledge.

**The Grantor**

THE "GRANTOR" IS THE person or entity that creates the trust initially and puts the property in the trust. The owner of the assets. The grantor's motivation is to get the real estate out of his name for either some or all of the following reasons. Asset protection, reduce frivolous lawsuits, elimination of probate, eliminate estate taxes, and anonymity.

Most land trusts are revocable (meaning the terms of the trust agreement can be changed). A land trust can also be created as irrevocable (meaning the terms of the land trust cannot be changed) but are not common with land trusts.

**The Trustee**

THE "TRUSTEE" IS ONLY a figurehead in a land trust. We only want the trustee to hold legal and equitable title to the real estate. A letter of direction to the trustee, from beneficiary, will instruct the trustee to act on any demands of the beneficiary. Therefore, you have complete control of what the trust does, as the beneficiary of the land trust.

The trustee is the person who will manage your trust assets. It can be a person, or even a corporate entity that you control, such as a corporation or LLC. The most important rule for a trustee in a land trust is to follow the instructions of the beneficiary.

Most people immediately think they are the most trustworthy person for their business interests, and they should be the trustee. But it's a bad idea to be your own trustee.

Designating yourself as a trustee will destroy anonymity, and therefore lose the greatest benefit of the land trust, which is privacy.

But you could set up an LLC to be the trustee, which you would control as the manager member of the LLC, and still have anonymity on the public record. The title would show the LLC as trustee of a trust.

The trustee has no power to act, without the written directions from the beneficiary. A trustee is required to act, only on the direction of the beneficiary, and the trustee is bound by the trust document, and has a duty to protect trust assets for the beneficiaries. The trustee manages, holds legal and equitable title of the land trust assets, and fulfills the duties called upon by the beneficiary.

Trustees are also subject to very strict standards as to the way in which their powers and discretions may be exercised. Whether or not a trustee is remunerated, he must act prudently in the management of trust property, and will be liable for breach of trust if, by failing to exercise proper care and follow directions of the beneficiaries.

There are over 100 years of case law that guarantees a trustee of a trust, that they are not personally responsible for their actions as a trustee (unless they commit fraud or act without direction from the beneficiary).

**The Trustee's Obligations to the Beneficiaries**

THE LAND TRUST AGREEMENT lists specific duties and obligations for the trustee. A brief summary of those obligations is:

1. To hold title to the property for the benefits of the beneficiaries.
2. To protect and conserve the property.
3. Not to reveal the identity of the beneficiaries.
4. Not to record the trust agreement in the public records.

5. To execute any legal documents without the direction of the beneficiaries.
6. To maintain records of the names and addresses of the beneficiaries.
7. To resign and hand over books and records if his activities are terminated.

**The Beneficiary**

THE "BENEFICIARY" IS the party to the land trust that benefits from the trust and has control over the land trust. A beneficiary in a land trust has total control in what the trust does. The authority to direct the trustee is called "written direction to trustee". You are entitled as the beneficiary, to any proceeds that the trust property generates from lease or sell of trust assets, or any way you decide to make a profit.

Important to remember that a beneficiary can be a person or an entity. For the maximum liability protection, an LLC is the best entity to protect you and the property as the beneficiary. The land trust is used for privacy. An assignment of beneficial interest from you to your LLC is private and not recorded. You control the LLC, as the beneficiary of the land trust.

See, I told you it wouldn't be that bad...LOL You passed your exam, let's move on.

# CHAPTER 14 How to Set Up a Land Trust

The land trust is simple to set up, operate, and administer. Setting up the land trust requires two things. An executed land trust agreement, and a deed "recorded" to the trustee. This can be done simultaneously at a closing, or by creating the land trust first, then deeding the property into the trust. The land trust must have the property deed recorded in the land trust's name, or trustee's name, on county records, to be a valid land trust.

**Transferring The Property into the Land Trust**

THE BEST WAY TO SET up a land trust is to do so when you are purchasing a property, and have the seller deed it directly to the trust. This way your name never appears in the public records. The other way to structure it is to buy it in your name and then deed it into the trust.

A person who already owns a property can easily transfer the property into a land trust by simply signing a deed to a trustee. Because it's in your name now and on public record, you will lose some secrecy. Public records will always show that the deed went from you to a trustee. But there are no taxes owed on the transfer, because it went into your land trust, and you are no longer the owner.

Transferring title to the trustee can take several forms. It can be a quitclaim deed or general warranty deed. It will usually read as (John Doe, Trustee of 123 Main Street, Trust.) The land trust will always give the beneficiary full power of direction to instruct the trustee in all duties. It is always best to use a warranty deed to transfer property into the trustee's name as the trustee of the land trust, giving full power and limitations to the trustee, as per trust agreement.

If you wish to keep your purchase price of the property secret, and not let the property appraiser or assessor know it was sold, (taxes may go up) then you should set up a land trust with the seller as the initial beneficiary. At closing, the seller will sign the trust, and then deed the property into the trust.

Since it is his own trust, there should be no record on the deed of a sales price, and no transfer tax on the deed. Then the seller immediately signs an assignment of beneficial interest to you, the buyer. You then become the owner of the property. Do not record the trust agreement in the public records under any circumstances.

There's a common mistake that investors make when using the land trust. You want to eliminate any personal connections you have to the land trust. By having the same mailing address as your personal residence, can be a dead give-away to any attorney searching to find if you have any ownership in the trust.

### Title to the Property

IN A TYPICAL LAND TRUST, both legal and equitable titles are vested in the trustee. The beneficiary has no interest in the real estate. What the beneficiary has is an interest in the trust. In some states this is spelled out in the statute, but in most states, it is not, so to create this arrangement, the trust agreement must state that the trustee holds equitable and legal title and the beneficiary merely has an interest in the "proceeds and avails" of the trust.

### Liability

BECAUSE THE BENEFICIARY has the duty to manage the property in a land trust, the beneficiary also has the liability for mismanagement. Thus, a trust is not insulation from lawsuits for negligence. For extra protection, the author recommends using an LLC, because it offers more liability protection.

A trustee should not be held personally liable for the debts, obligations, or liabilities of the trust. Unless of course, he does something illegal, and without the direction of the beneficiaries, such as running off with the property?

### What if I have a Mortgage?

THE GARN-ST. GERMAIN Depository Institutions Act of 1982 specifically allows one to place one's property into a (revocable) trust without triggering the due-on-sale clause. That means that one can transfer mortgaged property to a land trust without interference from the bank. This is the case as long as the borrower remains a beneficiary, the property consists of fewer than five dwelling units, the trust is revocable, and does not convey rights of occupancy to others.

The Garn-St. Germain Depository Act states: "a lender may not exercise its option pursuant to a due-on-sales clause upon a transfer into an intervivos trust in which the borrower is and remains a beneficiary and which does not relate to a transfer of rights of property."

Thus, the Garn-St. Germain Act freed individuals to put their property in a land trust for estate planning and anonymous property ownership without fear of lenders calling their loan due.

### Dealing With Hazard Insurance

SINCE TITLE TO YOUR property will not be in your name, you cannot technically be the owner and beneficiary of your hazard insurance policy. A transfer of title will usually void a hazard insurance policy. It is best, therefore, to notify your hazard insurance company

to name the land trust as a "loss payee" on your policy. and yourself as the beneficiary of the trust, as a loss payee, if needed. Call them to find out the best way to insure it.

### How To Avoid Fraudulent Transfers?

ASSET PROTECTION IS always needed in most circumstances. Protecting your assets from risk and liability is firmly established as a necessity in today's litigious society. But there comes a point in the law where financial transactions and legal proceedings are no longer allowed. This happens when a lawsuit is filed against you. Laws in every state prohibit the transfer of property intended to hinder, delay, or defraud a creditor in order to avoid paying an imminent legal obligation. The law also prohibits transfers that leave you unable to meet your foreseeable obligations.

Although the law prevents you from creating an asset protection plan to evade current debts, it does allow for asset protection planning to avoid liability from future unanticipated creditors.

As long as people have used real estate transactions, they have also attempted to conceal their ownership of property in order to defeat the claims of creditors.

To protect creditors from not being able to collect on their judgments, the courts have sought to invalidate transfers made with the intent to defraud creditors. Any transfer of property which is proved to be a "fraudulent conveyance" may be set aside by a court.

**Selling the Land Trust Property**

A PROPERTY IN A LAND trust can be sold in two ways. The first transaction would be for the trustee to deed the property out of the trust to the purchaser at closing, or the beneficiary can assign his beneficial interest in the trust to the purchaser, at closing.

At that time if the property is the only thing the trust owns, then the trust would end. But if the beneficial interest is assigned, then the buyer of the property becomes the new owner of the trust. The new buyer can keep the same trustee, or may want to have a new trustee appointed to the land trust.

**Deeding the Property Out of Trust**

IF THE PROPERTY IS to be deeded out of trust to the buyer, then the main documents that are needed are the contract for sale, the deed from the trustee, and direction to the trustee to sign the contract and deed at closing. As explained previously, the trustee can convey the property by either trustee's deed or warranty deed.

**Assigning the Beneficial Interest**

INSTEAD OF DEEDING the property and the buyer receiving a deed of the real estate from the trustee, a buyer can receive an assignment of the beneficial interest from the beneficiaries. In such cases the buyer would step into the shoes of the previous beneficiary of the land trust.

The advantage of buying the beneficial interest and then replacing the trustee, over having a deed from the seller's trustee to the buyer's trustee is that there is no public record of the sale. Thus, no record of sale or sales price, which could save on transfer taxes, and possibly keep the original financing terms on property.

**Changing Successor Beneficiaries**

A BENEFICIARY CAN CHANGE the successor beneficiary at any time. To do so an "Amendment to Trust" should be executed stating the change. No approval is needed from such previous successor beneficiaries. In most states this does not require witnesses, but is highly recommended to be notarized, to prove change of ownership if ever needed for proof and date of transfer in any kind of litigation ever arises.

# CHAPTER 15 Protecting your Personal Residence

There are a few important things to consider when protecting your home equity. First, what state do you live in? Does the state have a large homestead exemption? Every state provides some level of equity amount that a creditor can't take from you. For instance, if you live in Florida, you are exempt no matter how expensive your home is.

If someone gets a million-dollar judgment against you, they cannot take your home. But in some states the exemption is only twenty thousand. So, if you do not live in Florida, you need to protect the equity in your personal home.

Well, how do we protect our home? Any amount that an insurance policy does not cover in a judgment, will attach to your home and any other assets that you own. Your home is put at risk, by something that you have done, not what the house did. Let us say for example, that you are involved in a car accident. They sue you. The house did not get sued; you did. The judgment is against you for one million dollars, and they want to collect on it. So, then they're going after any asset that appears in your name.

Sometimes they do not try to directly take your home. They simply record the judgment in the county that your home is located in, and the judgment attaches to the property.

Now, when you go to refi or sell your home, the creditor knows he is going to get paid. On top of that, the judgment is growing at 10% statutory rates of interest. The longer you take to pay it off, the bigger the judgment gets.

So, how do we keep your home safe, and this from happening? Well, the first thing is to get your home out of your name. We do this with our land trust and by using a nominee name as the trustee. This could be a friend, attorney or an entity such as a limited liability company.

Let us say you set up an LLC to be the trustee of the land trust. The purpose of the LLC is to be the trustee for your land trust, and nothing else. You are the only member and have full control of the LLC, and you decide on what the LLC does. The name of your LLC is "Blue Sky LLC". Let us say you named your land trust the "Blue-Sky Trust".

The deed to your house would now read as follows, Blue Sky LLC as Trustee of Blue- Sky Trust. So now if you were personally sued and a creditor obtains a judgment against you, and they recorded the judgment in the county that your home resides in, your name does not show up as the owner. There is no judgment against your home because you no longer own the home, the Blue-Sky land trust now owns your home.

The second thing you can do if you choose to have an extra protected layer, is set up another LLC to hold the beneficial interest of your land trust, instead of you as the beneficiary.

This would give you liability protection if your land trust was ever sued. As the beneficiary of a land trust, you are still liable for what happens on the property, if there is a liability against the land trust. The liability is subject to what the land trust owns, and the beneficiary would not be you. That is why the land trust always need to be a payee on the homeowner's insurance policy, if the property is ever damaged or is subject to a liability that has occurred.

———————

ANOTHER LLC CAN NOW be used to own the land trust's beneficial interest. By transferring your beneficial interest of the land trust into an LLC, you now have liability protection and privacy. The LLC would be set up as a disregarded LLC, which means it doesn't need to file a tax return. But now, the land trust is owned by the LLC as the beneficiary, instead of you.

So now you have taken your beneficial interest of the land trust and assigned it to an LLC. You now have one LLC as the trustee, and the other LLC is the beneficiary of the land trust, instead of you personally being the beneficiary. You still have complete control of the land trust by the membership of the LLCs that have become the trustee and beneficiary of your land trust that owns your home.

No one knows except you, about the land trust or the LLCs, because it's private. None of the transfers are recorded, except the deed that shows the LLC as the owner. The transfer of your land trust's beneficial interest into an LLC, with an assignment of beneficial interest, is not recorded and not on any public record. Just remember, when setting up the LLC, use a different address than your home address, because of tax statements or any LLC statements being mailed. You don't need someone to know where you live. Just simply rent a mailbox for the return of statements.

Your home is now owned by the land trust with one LLC as a trustee, which will be recorded, and the second LLC holds the beneficial interest of the land trust that is not recorded. This gives you complete anonymity and control of your home without another person being a beneficiary. You are the only member of the LLCs and have complete control of all aspects of this special arrangement that protects the equity in your home. You simply sign the LLC documents as needed as the only member and owner.

# CHAPTER 16 Sixteen Reasons for a Land Trust

### Circumventing Lending Guidelines

Certain types of loans, (such as HUD 203k Investor Loans) set forth guidelines which limit the amount of units an remove the liability from the credit report, you may consider having the trustee execute an assumption package on behalf of the trust if the loans are an assumed FHA or VA loan used in the purchase of the real estate.

### 1. Ease of Foreclosure

AN INSTALLMENT LAND contract is an owner-financed arrangement in which the seller holds legal title, and the buyer makes payments to the seller. The buyer has an equitable title.

This arrangement is similar to an installment sales agreement such as a car loan, with the exception of you can't repossess the real estate without court intervention which is timely and expensive.

While in most states the foreclosure of a real estate mortgage or a deed of trust requires lengthy court proceedings and gives the owner a right of redemption, a beneficial interest given as collateral can often be recovered much more quickly. When the beneficial interest in a land trust is given as collateral (security agreement), a collateral assignment of the beneficial interest, and a UCC-1 financing statement are used as security.

In such cases, the foreclosure is handled under the Uniform Commercial Code and is a much simpler procedure than a real estate foreclosure. Also, there's no up-set bid period at the auction, as with a standard deed of trust, that could delay the foreclosure.

**2. Circumventing the "Due-on-Sale" Clause**

THE DUE-ON-SALE CLAUSE is a clause in a mortgage that gives the lender the right to declare the full amount of the mortgage due. Most people are not aware that all mortgages and deeds of trusts have a little clause buried in the small print that reads in part.

"If all or any part of the property herein is transferred without the lender's prior written consent, the lender may require all sums secured hereby immediately due and payable."

The Garn-St. Germain Depository Institutions Act was an initiative of the Regan administration meant "to revitalize the housing industry by strengthening the financial stability of home mortgages lending institutions and ensuring the availability of home mortgage loans.

The legal term for this language is an "acceleration clause." The clause gives the lender the option to demand full payment of the loan amount due. It is only an option and the lender has the ability to call the loan due but is not required to. The due-on-sale clause can be invoked by a lender who wants to collect the full balance of a property holder's outstanding debt if the owner chooses to sell the property, without paying the loan off.

But there's an exclusion in the act that will allow a property owner to place his property into an intervivos trust without triggering the due on sale clause. Once a property is placed into a land trust, the beneficiary of the land trust can be changed without any public record. This can change the ownership of the property without the bank's knowledge of an ownership transfer.

Remember, the bank wants their loan payment, and not the property. They rarely apply the due on sale clause if payments are being made regularly on the property. If an individual is making required payments, enacting the due on sale clause and possibly foreclosing on a property doesn't make sense. The banks really don't care who is making payments, as long as they are made on time. Most will pretend they do not know about any change of ownership, as long as they are getting their payments and it's insured with them as loss payee.

Don't make the mistake of calling the banks and asking for permission to transfer ownership. This alerts the bank of what is going on, and their bank regulations could then force them into calling the loan due if there was ever a change of ownership.

**3. Land Trusts May Avoid Transfer Taxes**

A LAND TRUST WILL NOT help you avoid paying taxes entirely. But it does open the door to certain tax benefits that are not usually realized. For example, the documentary stamp tax or transfer tax can be avoided by using a land trust because the land is not transferred.

It stays in the name of the same trustee while the beneficial ownership of the trust is changed and this transfer is not taxable. On large commercial properties this can save tens of thousands of dollars, because the property is not reassessed when sold, because there is no deed recording of the change of beneficial interest of the trust.

1. Land Trust Allows You to Remain Anonymous

Real estate that is managed as a land trust will be associated with the trustee's name in public records. If you are concerned with anyone knowing you are the true owner, this is the best way to keep your name out of the public eye.

**5. Land Trusts Protects You from Liability**

WHEN YOU BUY A PROPERTY, the purchase shows to the public, along with the amount you paid. Unfortunately, in today's world there is no way to avoid someone researching your purchase at the courthouse records.

All it takes is for someone to scroll through the records of the county recorder, calculate your net worth, and make a move to sue you. By putting your property into a land trust, you do not wn it. You can look broke to anyone with intentions of filing a lawsuit against you for a quick payout.

**6. Land Trusts Keeps the Price a Secret**

A LAND TRUST CAN KEEP certain financial information out of the public record. In many cases this anonymity can help give you leverage. If you are negotiating a deal, obscuring your net worth or the prices you have paid for other pieces of property can come in handy. This is especially applicable to real estate investors working in high profile commercial real estate where negotiations can be extremely difficult and public knowledge of your financial profile can be a liability in the negotiations.

**7. Land Trusts Prevents Liens and Judgments**

A PROPERTY CAN BE OWNED by several different investors. Placing the property into a land trust can protect the investors in the event of a justified lawsuit. Creditors or litigants will not be able to go after the assets of individual investors just because they are partial owners of the property as being beneficiaries of the land trust. Keep in mind that even lawsuits that have nothing to do with the property can be an issue if a judgment is rendered against an owner, or partner of the same jointly owned property.

The judgment will automatically attach to any property owned by the defendant. A land trust can prevent these kinds of misfortunes from impacting any other investors in the group and it can make it easier to deflect these issues away from the property owned by the land trust.

Simply stated, a lien judgment against the owner personally, can't attach to a property in a land trust, because it's not in his name.

### 8. Land Trusts Help Minimize the Difficulty of Probate

PROBATE IS THE PROCESS whereby the assets of a deceased person are parceled out the legal next of kin, especially in the absence of a will. The probate process can be long, drawn-out, costly and emotionally draining on a family that has suffered a loss. This process is public record and can be researched by anyone who is curious of who got what from deceased assets. If creditors or family members who feel entitled to the property want to lay claim to the landed assets, they can weigh down the whole procedure in painful arguments and court litigations.

### 9. Land Trusts Make It Easy to Transfer Property

PLACING LANDED ASSETS into a land trust can make them much easier to transfer, as long as both the grantor and the beneficiary are still alive. In some states, a trust will help avoid paying out transfer taxes that could greatly burden the whole exchange.

In structuring the sale of a property with the right legal instruments, you can minimize your losses and maximize your profits with the land trust.

### 10. Choosing the Trustee

SELECTING A TRUSTEE is a very important part of the overall land trust creation process. Taking time to choose the right person is necessary because they'll have fiduciary duties, as well as management responsibilities, over your trust assets. I always suggest it's best to use a knowledgeable attorney that charges a small annual fee to be the trustee of your trust. You also receive attorney-client privilege benefits with this action.

### 11. Using an LLC as the Beneficiary of the Land Trust

WHEN SETTING UP YOUR land trust you can determine who or what entity will be the beneficiary of the trust. To attain maximum asset protection, I recommend using an LLC to be the beneficiary of the land trust.

This gives you the liability protection that only the statutes of an LLC can provide. By simply assigning the land trust's beneficial interest from you into an LLC, you now retain all the liability protection that an LLC offers for both inside and outside liability protection for you and the property.

In the real world it's important to understand where a lawsuit may come from, and the concept of inside and outside liability. Inside liability is a lawsuit risk that is produced by the real estate itself. A tenant falls or something bad happens on the property that causes you to be sued. A lawsuit over these types of claims creates some amount of jeopardy for your other properties and any assets you own. Anything in your personal name can be loss, in the event of a lawsuit.

The first defense in asset protection planning is to insulate and shield yourself from any liability arising out of the property, so that you don't expose your other assets to this lawsuit claim.

Outside liability is the risk of other activities, such as running a business, or being in an auto accident.

A lawsuit from these sources poses a potential threat to all of your assets, including the equity in your properties. The second objective of asset protection planning is to protect the properties and all your assets from outside risks that may come from a different path, such as an auto accident.

**12. Using an LLC as Beneficiary**

AN LLC DOES NOT HAVE the rigid paperwork required to maintain formal minutes and resolutions, by a corporation like an S or C Corporation. Record-keeping requirements can be minimized without a threat of the members being sued individually.

Unlike a corporation that can have the corporate veil pierced and cause a loss of liability protection, if the proper paperwork is not maintained by the corporation.

### 13. No Tax Return with the Land Trust

THE LAND TRUST DOES not require a separate tax return or a separate tax identification number. The trust is transparent to the taxing authorities. The beneficiary of the land trust reports the income and expenses on his tax return just as if the trust did not exist.

If you transfer your currently owned property to a land trust, no tax event occurs. Your basis and tax reporting remain the same. Your ownership of real estate in a land trust does not affect your ability to accomplish tax deferred exchanges. Beneficiary of the land trust includes persons, corporations, partnerships, limited partnerships, or other trusts such as a living trust.

For tax purposes the land trust is disregarded and all taxable activities of the trust are reported on the returns of the beneficiaries. These returns may be individual, partnership or corporate, depending upon the filing status of the beneficiaries.

An LLC may file corporate or partnership returns, depending on how the members have structured the LLC for tax purposes.

### 14. Avoiding Partition

IN MOST STATES WHEN property is owned jointly by two or more persons any one of them may go to court and require partition, which means the property is put up for auction by a court. The proceeds are then divided among the owners. A disgruntled family member could ruin the progress of a development or construction, because of a disagreement.

Property held in a land trust is not subject to partition, and must be authorized and agreed upon to sell by all beneficiaries.

**15. Avoiding Seasoning Problems**

SEASONING IS THE LENGTH of time a property has been owned in the name of the owner. Some lenders require a property to be held for a certain length of time before it can be financed and resold, or length of time before the lender will finance it for a new buyer Using a land trust can allow a property to stay with the same land trust trustee, while the beneficial interest is being sold, which would not be recorded in public records.

# CHAPTER 17 A Land Trust is Different

I want to make sure there's no confusion about an estate planning living trust, and a real estate land trust. Let's examine what each trust is, and its duties as a trust. Both a "land trust" and the typical estate planning "living trust", are both revocable trusts but there is where the similarities end. With the exceptions that both can be used to avoid probate, and both or formed during the grantor's lifetime.

A living trust usually has the same trustee and beneficiary, and is designed to do what a will does. It's basically an extension of a will, without the probate process. But the important difference between a will, is a will goes through probate, and a living trust avoids probate. A living trust is a box that holds everything that could be in a will, which could include the beneficial interest of a land trust, to avoid probate at the owner's death.

This is the main reason to have an estate planning living trust. It saves money and time upon the beneficiary's death, by avoiding probate. An expensive and time-consuming process required by the court system to distribute assets according to a will. You do not want your assets to be distributed to heirs by a will. Use a living trust to prevent probate fees and excess time that assets will be tied up in court.

The living trust usually has a trust name that is named after the grantor, such as ("Mary Jane's Living Trust"). It is designed to hold many different assets besides real estate, and provide the transfer of assets at one's death, and avoid probate. The major legal term that differentiates a living trust from a land trust is the way title is classified with the trustee.

The living trust gives legal title to the trustee, and a land trust gives both legal and equitable title to a trustee. By doing this, the land trust's beneficiary holds no real property interest in the property, only a beneficial interest in the land trust. Simply put, real estate liens can attach to a beneficiary in a living trust, but no real estate liens will attach to the beneficiary of a land trust.

In a living trust, the trustee holds legal title to the land, and the beneficiary of the living trust holds equitable title. And the living trust's beneficial interest is considered real property. Because the beneficiary's interest is real property, real estate liens will attach to the property that's in a living trust, but (NOT) a land trust, in the event of a lawsuit.

The antithesis of a living trust is the investor's land trust. It is designed to give privacy and anonymity to real estate ownership. With a land trust only the trustee and the name of the trust are known to the public, that's listed on the deed. The deed to the property is held in the name of the trustee only, and the trust agreement is (**NOT**) recorded in any public record.

The land trust's "name" usually has a generic name, such as the address of the property it holds, such as ("123 Anywhere Street, Raleigh, NC.") The land trust is ideally created to hold one property, "per land trust". A land trust can also avoid probate by transferring assets and save on administrative expenses, upon death, with a named successor beneficiary. The land trust can then carry on as usual or can end the trust on death of beneficiary. Set up a separate land trust for each property.

In a land trust, the trustee holds both legal and equitable title to the land and the

beneficiary's interest is considered (**PERSONAL PROPERTY.**) This gives the land trust benefits over the living trust, because of the beneficiary's interest is now considered personal property and not real property. A personal lien against you will not attach to the property in a land trust. This will allow you to sell the property without paying off the lien.

Here are two benefits of using a land trust where the beneficiary's interest is personal property. There are many more benefits in using land trusts.

Judgments against the beneficiaries of land trusts are not liens on real property. This is because the beneficiary's interest is considered personal property and not real property.

If a beneficiary dies and does not pay death taxes the taxes do not create a lien on the property that must be paid off before the house is sold. This is because the beneficiaries' interest is defined as personal property and not real property.

Finally, because conveyance of the trust property is made solely by the trustee, a land trust can prevent many of the delays associated with transfers of property held in traditional trusts or other forms of multiple ownership.

For example, delays created by the death, incapacity, bankruptcy, litigation, divorce or no residency of one or more beneficiaries may be avoided by having a land trust hold the property, with instructions in the trust agreement for any successor beneficiaries.

A living trust can then be used, to be the final box that holds all assets, including all land trust's beneficial interests, money, bank accounts, brokage accounts. This would then avoid the expensive process of probate and the assets can be immediately transferred to heirs.

Don't forget, an estate "Will" is always probated. A living trust under all state laws avoids probate and the expense and time associated with probate courts. Estate attorney fees and debts can substantially add up and reduce the value of the estate with probate costs, before being transferred to heirs.

# CHAPTER 18 Preventing a Medicaid Lien

Many of us will face the day, if not already when a family member will require long-term care in a nursing home. For most, a home is the largest asset that a person owns. Not only is it their largest asset, but it's also most likely the single biggest purchase made in their lifetimes. Raising a family, collecting memories throughout a lifetime creates a home filled with a desire to leave with children or grandchildren, so that they may also experience similar joy and memories with their own families.

However, if one of the family members needs long-term care in a nursing home and lacks the means to pay for such services, then they will need to apply for Medicaid to cover the cost. Nursing home assisted living is very, very expensive. The way the system works now, is you're essentially required to spend through all of your assets, and then when you're well below the poverty level then Medicaid will start paying for your care.

The way that Medicaid works, if you want to enroll in the long-term caravan, they have what's called a 5-year look-back period. So, they go back five years to see if you have gifted any assets to a trust, or individual. If you did, they can undo it, like it never happened. Because they don't want to pay for the long-term care, and then have no way to recoup their money back, if there's no assets to liquidate.

If a family member qualifies, Medicaid will pay the cost for long-term care in a nursing home. The cost per month could reach up to $25,000 or more and leave a total bill in the range of hundreds of thousands of dollars owed to Medicaid.

Most people don't realize that once Medicaid begins paying the cost of long-term care, it is required to seek recovery for any payments made on the Medicaid recipient's home. This is done by placing a lien against the property. The lien guarantees repayment if the real estate is sold during the lifetime of the Medicaid recipient. If the property is not sold during the recipient's lifetime, Medicaid may then seek repayment from the recipient's assets in the probate estate after his or her death. You can lose all the equity that was generated by the value of the property.

Because the cost of care is so expensive, a Medicaid lien can quickly wipe out the equity in the home in a very short period. The primary residence of an individual receiving long-term care in a nursing home is exempt from a Medicaid lien if the spouse of the Medicaid recipient is still living in the home.

However, the primary residence is only exempt from Medicaid if the relative lives in the home. If the spouse of the relative also needs long-term care and enters a nursing home or passes away, Medicaid may then place a lien on the home because the spouse no longer lives there.

This is why it is so important to place a home in a trust to remove ownership as soon as possible before nursing care is needed and qualify for Medicaid before the 5-year look- back. A living trust can be the beneficiary of a land trust, and hold all assets to avoid any probate at death.

Before utilizing any planning techniques, it is strongly recommended that you should consult an elder law attorney to discuss the best available options for the situation. With proper planning you can avoid potentially losing your home to Medicaid liens and repayment obligations.

The primary residence of an individual receiving long-term care in a nursing home is exempt from a Medicaid lien if the spouse of the Medicaid recipient is still living in the home. However, the primary residence is only exempt from a lien as long as the spouse lives in the home.

If the spouse also needs long-term care and enters a nursing home or passes. Medicaid may then place a lien on the home because the spouse no longer lives there. Again, it is highly advised to consult with an elder law attorney for the best available options on preventing a Medicaid lien from attaching to the property.

# CHAPTER 19 Disadvantages of a Land Trust

The problem with land trusts is that they have no asset protection against liability. If you have a beneficial interest in a land trust, and it is discovered you hold this asset, and a lawsuit is awarded against you personally, your beneficial interest could be attached.

The plaintiff's attorney could then file for a writ of execution against your beneficial interest in the land trust. The beneficial interest can be taken from you and the attorney can take control of the trust and gain control of its assets. This is why anonymity is important with using a land trust.

Another problem with land trusts is that they do not protect you from what happens inside of the trust. For instance, you have a tenant that has a slip and fall and sues the land trust. Through the process of the plaintiff's attorney discovery, he finds out who the beneficiary is. He then tries to attach your beneficial interest in the trust.

This is another important reason in using an LLC, as the beneficiary of the land trust. Because the trust is a self-settled trust that's revocable, you do not have any asset protection. A judge could simply order you to put the property back in your personal name.

That is why you should always use a "Limited Liability Company" as the beneficiary of the land trust for maximum liability protection. This is simply done by setting up a LLC, and then transferring your beneficial interest in the land trust to your LLC with an "Assignment of Beneficial Interest". This assignment of beneficial interest is not recorded but needs to be notarized to prove the date, if the land trust is ever sued.

**Some Paperwork Needed**

A LAND TRUST REQUIRES keeping up with the paperwork. A trust agreement must be drafted and executed, a new deed must be filed, insurance payees must be placed on all insurance, tax records address mailings must be kept separate, and the trustee must keep books and records

Basically, once the land trust is in place and a trustee is recorded as the trustee of the land trust on public record, you can place the trust agreement in your file cabinet and forget about it. The problem you will encounter, is to find attorneys that are familiar with land trusts, because most of them do not understand land trusts.

**Stepping Out of the Land Trust to Refinance Property**

IF YOU GO TO REFINANCE the property after placing the property in trust, most lenders may require that you produce the trust agreement, or "step out" of the trust and put the title back into your personal name. You can then transfer the property back into trust, but this will leave a paper trail for potential creditors to follow. But you can once again after refinancing the property, place it back in the land trust and have the beneficial interest assigned to an LLC for privacy and liability protection.

**Loss of Homestead Protection**

SOME STATES HAVE HOMESTEAD protection laws that protect seizure and sale of their property by creditors. They only afford the protection, of course, to the owner's personal residence, and depending on what state determines the amount of protection. A transfer of property into trust may result in the loss of homestead protection, since the grantor of the property is no longer the owner of any legal or equitable interest in the real estate.

You may want to check with an attorney that's familiar with homestead protection before any transfer to trust.

You can see why the benefits of using a land trust far outweigh any disadvantages of using the land trust for the first rung on the ladder of asset protection.

If you live in the state of Florida, it gives you complete homestead protection regardless of the value of your personal residence. So, a land trust is not needed for your personal residence. Florida is one of the few states that have land trust statues on its state regulations that gives great benefits of using a land trust to protect all your investment properties.

# CHAPTER 20 LLC for Asset Protection

What are the advantages of a "Limited Liability Company," known as an LLC? When you form an LLC, you form a new person, a legal person created by statute. It is a company that's created to give liability protection to its owners. Owners of an LLC are listed as members. An LLC can be listed as two types of LLC. It can be member- managed, or manager-managed LLCs. Both members and managers do not have any personal liability for the LLCs debts or liabilities.

In our lawsuit-plagued world, using an LLC to separate you personally from all the potential liability is almost a legal necessity. Year after year, thousands of people lose nearly everything they have due to personal liability. People give the excuse that they don't need an LLC because I have insurance.

I'm afraid you are in for a rude awakening, if you think insurance is going to cover all lawsuits that might arise out of your dealings. Insurance will not protect you from most lawsuits that happen regarding most actions in real estate investing. Especially, when dealing in business contracts.

This includes buying and selling real estate, leasing to a tenant, and dealing with contractors on rehabbing, or any service, for that matter. The only thing that's going to save your butt, and your hard-earned dollars, is an asset protection entity called an LLC to shield you from inside and outside liability. Please remember, a personal lawsuit against you, regardless of how much insurance you have, is going to involve a lot of wasted time and pain in your life.

Let's see for example, how we can use a land trust in conjunction with an LLC, to not only give us anonymity, but also protect us against liability, in the event of a lawsuit. The way we do that is to combine the trust with an LLC to create this secret asset shield.

So, you now own an asset inside of a land trust with a nominee trustee, such as an attorney. And the land trust is owned by an LLC, that provides liability protection, and the land trust adds anonymity. The property is now invisible and protected against liability, with the privacy that only a land trust can give.

Furthermore, if anyone is looking, that attorney trustee now gives you (Attorney-Client Privilege.) The attorney can't provide any information legally, because that information is protected by the "attorney-client privilege." If there is ever a lawsuit, they must sue through the trust. What they then find out is the trust is owned by an LLC.

So, the most you can ever lose from that lawsuit, is that single asset inside of that LLC. For example, if a land trust held a property, and was owned by the LLC, and someone was hurt on the property, and they sued the LLC, depending on state LLC laws, they possibly could get the property. But not the personal assets of the members or managers of the LLC.

### Assigning the Beneficial Interest to an LLC

IT IS EASILY DONE WITH a simple one-page assignment that is not recorded, but needs to be notarized. It then goes into your file cabinet with the trust agreement. If for some reason the bank wants to see the land trust agreement, for example, when refinancing the property, you need to show the bank only the trust agreement showing you as the beneficiary of the trust, and NOT the assignment of beneficial interest to the LLC.

If you want to refinance a property held in a land trust, do not show the bank your assignment of beneficial interest to the LLC. This would show that the LLC owns the land trust, instead of you. Because of this, they may not refinance the property in the LLCs name, as the loan is going from a residential loan to a commercial loan. It's important that the assignment of the beneficial interest is not recorded and needs to stay in the file cabinet with the land trust agreement.

But by placing the properties in a land trust first, and then assigning the beneficiary interest into an LLC, there is no record of the LLC. The name of the trustee is the only record that shows on the recorded deed. This avoids the ability to search the properties at the Secretary of State's website. Land trusts are especially a good idea in case you own more than one property and don't want anyone to know you own more properties.

### Positive Cash Flow

AN IMPORTANT CONSIDERATION when evaluating how many properties to title to an LLC, is the cash flow that these properties generate.

Take for instance, if a property was generating $450.00 per month, and you had four of these in one LLC.

That would be $1800.00 per month of cash flow that the one LLC would be at risk of losing.

That would be a very precipitous loss of cash flow that would affect most people's source of income. But if there's only one property per LLC, then that would be the only one at risk from a judgment, and you would still maintain the cash flow on the other properties.

Losing one $450.00 property would be a lot easier to deal with, than losing the whole

$1800.00 stream of cash flow. Important to remember, one land trust and one LLC for each separate property for maximum protection for all real estate assets.

# CHAPTER 21 LLC Member Benefits

Most business entities available under United States laws are designed to limit the liability of owners in certain ways, but only one puts that purpose in its name, "The Limited Liability Company". The LLC first became available in Wyoming in 1977.

The owners of an LLC are called "members". The LLC can be owned by one person called a single member LLC, or owned by two or more people that's called a multi- member LLC. The LLC is created by filing a state form called "Articles of Organization." This form is different in each state and can usually be found by going online to the Secretary of State's website to download.

When a person forms a corporation or LLC, it's for personal asset protection. This is called a corporate veil with using a corporation and an LLC veil using an LLC. An LLC is simpler to form, than a corporation, and is the number one business entity for asset protection. The LLC forms a protective wall between your business and your personal assets. If your LLC is sued, creditors can only attack the assets inside the LLC (what it owns) to settle the lawsuit.

It cannot go after your personal assets, such as personal bank accounts, or other assets that you own, outside the LLC. Every state has a separate LLC stature. In effect, all members in an LLC are considered limited partners. It provides the members flexible options for management and control. An LLC can be managed by all members, or one or more managers (who may not be members). Members can be given voting or non- voting status, and can have the power to remove and replace the LLC manager.

LLCs have become the leader in liability protection against lawsuits. When property is placed in an LLC, it can reduce personal exposure to risks surrounding that property. There are also several tax advantages. If you place real estate into a land trust and transfer the land trust's beneficial interest into an LLC, then it's no longer directly the owner's assets, and the property is protected by the LLC's state statutes.

**Assets the LLC Can Protect**

ALMOST ANYTHING CAN be titled to an LLC, such as vacation homes, rental properties, cars, boats, etc. This also includes businesses, equipment, and any physical assets. The liability protection would be in effect, unless you are personally involved in causing an accident.

You can take parts of a business and break it up into LLCs. Such, as having a service business that leases equipment to operate the business. The service business could be one LLC that holds nothing else, and the other LLC owns the equipment. If the service business gets sued, it owns nothing for the creditor to attach, because the equipment is owned by another LLC.

For instance, if your friend borrowed your boat and went skiing, and accidently hit another boat, and caused an accident, he will be sued for causing the accident. But you owned the boat, because you are the owner, you will be sued also, even if you had nothing to do with the accident.

But if an LLC owned the boat, and you had nothing to do with causing the accident, only the LLC will be sued, not you personally. A judgment against the LLC, could get the value of the boat, but none of your personal assets outside of the LLC. The same would apply to equipment, vehicles, jet skis, or anything that someone could operate and cause an accident.

### Member-Managed vs Manager-Managed LLC

WHEN FORMING AN LLC, you must decide whether it will be (**member-managed**) or (**manager-managed**). An LLC can either be managed by its members, called a member- managed LLC, or by its managers, called a manager-managed LLC.

A member-managed LLC is when all the LLC members (owners) can bind the LLC with contracts and agreements, as well as take part in the day-to-day business and operations. Most small LLCs that only have a few members, are member- managed.

A manager-managed LLC is when one, or a few designated people (called managers), can bind the LLC with contracts and agreements, as well as run the business and day-to-day business operations. The members do not have the authority to make decisions in the LLC, except appoint a manager to run the LLC.

**Single Member vs Multi-Member LLC**

LET'S SAY YOU HAVE one LLC with one owner (single member). The problem with a single- member LLC is that some jurisdictions have made it clear in case law in most states, a single- member LLC does not entitle the LLC member to a charging order protection. Because there's no one else but you, that holds a membership, or ownership in the LLC.

To receive the maximum liability protection from an LLC, you would make the LLC a **multi-member LLC,** not a **single-member LLC.** By adding another LLC member to the LLC, which could be a family member, trust agreement, or a family limited partnership, you now have a multi-member LLC, that would be taxed as a partnership and qualify for **charging order protection** in all states.

**Charging Order Protection**

ALL INVESTMENT REAL estate should be owned by an LLC, either through a land trust with the LLC holding the beneficiary interest of the trust, or the LLC directly holding title to the property. Property owned by the LLC cannot be claimed by your personal creditors because the property is owned by the LLC, rather than you are personally. Your personal creditors also cannot seize your membership interest in the LLC. Your personal creditors can only get a charging order against your membership interest.

The charging order liens whatever future distributions are paid to you from the LLC. As the LLC manager, you are not liable personally for LLC debt. Therefore, LLCs are preferable to limited partnerships to title investment real estate, because general partners of a limited partnership are personally liable for limited partnership debts. This problem can always be solved by using an LLC as the general partner in a limited partnership. The limited partnership can be another hurdle in the asset protection plan, when in conjunction with the LLC.

A charging order protection is a remedy that a creditor has to pursue the distributions that a member would receive from an LLC. So, if an LLC decides to distribute out money at the end of the year, and a creditor has a charging order against one of the members, then the creditor if the distribution stands, the creditor stands in the members shoes and takes the distribution.

If a charging order protection is ordered by a court directing an LLC's managers to pay to the judgment plaintiff, the debtor member's profits that would be distributed to the LLC member, would not be paid as a distribution. The charging order protection gives the financial rights, but not the legal authority to order the LLC to pay any distribution subject to the charging order protection.

Thus, the creditor ends up with nothing because he can't order the LLC to make any distributions to the members, because of the LLC's charging order protection laws. Additionally, the judgment creditor is obligated under the IRS Revenue Ruling 77-137 to report and pay taxes on their share of income, regardless if they received the income.

An outside judgment against one member, will not affect other members that are owners of the same LLC. In some states, obtaining a charging order is a creditor's exclusive remedy.

These states provide the greatest protection for LLC owners. Other states simply state that a charging order is an allowed remedy for creditors and allow foreclosure of the LLCs assets. Then the creditor is allowed to foreclose on the members interest and take over the ownership. This seldomly happens because the foreclosed interest has to be sold and has little value in this position for the bidder.

Creditors of an LLC member cannot seize or force a sale of the member's interest. Nor can the member's creditor vote the interest of the debtor-member. The member's creditor can only obtain a charging order remedy to direct the LLC to pay to the creditor any income distributions that would otherwise flow to the debtor-member.

This is the same charging order remedy that a limited partner's creditor has against an interest in a family limited partnership. The creditor gains only the financial rights of the debtor-member, not control or ownership rights.

There are two important distinctions of a charging order that limits what a creditor can do. First, it will not give voting rights, and second, force the LLC manager to pay distributions to a member or his creditor. The charging order only directs distributions to the creditor rather than the debtor-member.

If you manage your LLC, you are the one that will decide when you will make distributions. Your judgment creditor cannot replace you as the manager, because your creditor cannot vote. And if your creditor has a charging order against you, you can refuse to pay distributions.

As a member, you can pull the money out of the LLC without paying distributions. You can create a loan to you from the LLC, you can pay yourself a salary, and if you manage the LLC, you can pay yourself a manager's fee. None of this is considered a distribution, and your creditor cannot garnish loans or other forms of compensation that you may pay to yourself as the manager or member of your LLC.

The charging order creditor may be required to pay your income tax on LLC profits. Since an LLC is ordinarily taxed as a partnership, its tax liability automatically passes to its members.

The charging order creditor then, under certain circumstances, gets the tax bill for the debtor-member's share of LLC profits. This forces the member's creditor to pay taxes on the member's earnings, even if the creditor has not received any distributions.

That's a lose-lose proposition for any creditor. Finally, for protection, your LLC should have one or more members in addition to the one who is a lawsuit defendant. The courts are more hesitant to expand upon a creditor's remedy when other LLC members would be affected. Some courts will liquidate an LLC for the benefit of a creditor where the debtor is the only member, and no other members will be affected.

**The Limited Liability Company Act**

* A limited liability company is a legal entity separate from its members.

* Limited liability companies can be profit or nonprofit.

* SOME STATES ALLOW one-member liability companies, others require two or more members.

* A member may transfer his or her interest in future distributions and returns of capital.

* Managers and members of a limited liability company have limited liability.

* Limited liability companies can be for a fixed or perpetual date.

* Limited liability company operating agreements may not: 1) unreasonably restrict member's right to inspect company records: 2) eliminate or reduce a member's duty, loyalty, care or good faith when dealing with or on behalf of the company to expel a member convicted of wrongdoing, breaching the operating agreement or making it impractical for the limited liability company to carry on business with such a member.

* You can avoid double taxation with a limited liability company. Since the limited liability company is not a corporation, you can avoid corporate income tax if you choose.

Income from the limited liability company can be taxed personally to its members with a partnership.

# Chapter 22 LLC Operating Agreement

This LLC operating agreement is a legally binding business agreement that gives directions to the LLC on what it can do and not do. An LLC does not have to have an operating agreement to be legal, except for five states, but it's highly recommended to have one, regardless of what state. It entails the ownership of its members and how the company is managed and structured.

It can provide details such as when meetings are held, naming a registered agent, and selecting managers. It can tell the ownership percentage of its members and add or drop members. The operating agreement is not required to be recorded in any state, but just available if needed, with the five states that require it in their LLC general statutes.

Chances are, if you have a multi-member LLC, you want to keep the peace with your business partners. You want to understand who's going to be responsible for what's in your business, and you want to virtually eliminate the possibility of personal liability in the event you get sued.

By drafting your operating agreement, you're basically drafting the rules that you have chosen to follow in terms of how your LLC is going to be governed to your personal situation, if they don't contradict the state's LLC statutes.

An LLC will be governed by the state's LLC in which it resides. The operating agreement can define how it will be structured as to taxes. It defines how the company's profits and assets are allocated and distributed. It defines and sets out the agreements between the company's members. Members of the LLC are not personally liable or responsible for business debts and liabilities.

There are only five states that require that an LLC have an operating agreement. They are California, New York, Missouri, Maine, and Delaware. Even if you live in those states, an operating agreement is not required to be recorded on record with the LLC. You just need to have it signed by all members and have it on your books, computer, or file cabinet, and available if needed. If the LLC is a single member, the agreement needs to be signed by the single member.

There are several reasons why someone with an LLC needs an operating agreement. I strongly encourage you to have an operating agreement with any LLC that is formed. Number one, it strengthens the corporate veil that gives you the liability protection in an LLC, in the event you get sued.

An important clause to have in your operating agreement, is that if any member of the LLC is personally sued, the only remedy for the creditor is a charging order against the member's LLC interest. This limits the creditor's ability in most states, to foreclose on the LLC assets. In a well drafted LLC operating agreement, you can exclude a creditor from ever becoming a member or a partner of the LLC.

The best a creditor can get is the charging order. As stated above, the charging order is a limited right to receive uncertain future distributions of which an LLC member would be entitled to. Rarely, under regular circumstances, will a judge break up a company or force it to distribute distributions to a creditor.

**Main Provisions in an LLC Operating Agreement**

* PREAMBLE THE PREAMBLE dates and defines the agreement in includes the place of formation of the LLC operating agreement.

* Recitals The recitals provide the basic information of the company. For example, when and why the LLC was formed, such as being part of a joint venture, or if the LLC operating agreement is being amended and restated.

* Definitions LLC operating agreement can be a long document, so it is a good idea to define the terms that are commonly grouped together for clarity.

* Organization Matters This section includes the background details about the LLC, such as addresses of the members, where the LLC was formed, the LLC's registered agent, its location of its principal office, the term duration of the LLC, and the business purpose.

* Members and LLC Interests This section of the agreement includes matters relating to its members of the LLC, and their LLC interests. This section also provides information on any additional members and their liability.

* Management LLCs are managed by either one of its members (called a managing member), or a separate manager or board of managers. Managers

are responsible for strategic decisions, and the day-to-day operation of the company.

* Capital Contributions A capital contribution is the invested money or payment, that a member makes to an LLC in exchange for its LLC interests. In addition to showing the capital contributions of each member to the LLC, this section usually includes other provisions relating to the capital contribution such as, obligations to make contributions, how additional contributions are called, (capital call), provisions governing member loans to the company, and the consequences of a default on a mandatory capital contribution.

* LLC Termination an LLC can be terminated when the expiration of a specific term established in the LLC operating agreement has been reached, by the consent of its members, a decree of dissolutions, or the sale of the company. Allocations and distributions are set up in the LLC operating agreement. Profit and losses are allocated among the members, and how and when the company funds are actually distributed to the members.

* Eight Important Provisions in an LLC Operating Agreement.

1. Set LLC up as Manager Managed,

unless you are going to set up another LLC to own this LLC for anonymity. Such as a Wyoming LLC, then the Wyoming LLC would be Manager Managed and the in-state LLC "the state where property is located" would be Member Managed, which is solely

owned by the Wyoming LLC.

1. No Forced Distributions
2. No Pro Rata Distributions
3. No Charging Language
4. Restrictions on Transfers
5. Tax Provisions In line with LLC
6. No Right to Return Capital
7. No Appointment of Officers

# CHAPTER 23 Apartment Building Protection

Let's examine the benefits available from a land trust used in conjunction with an LLC. Let's look at a typical arrangement where John and Mary first owned the apartment building in their personal name. Now, let's examine the benefits when they place the property into a land trust, with a nominee trustee, and make the beneficiary of the land trust, an LLC.

First, there's no record of them on the real estate title. When a title search is performed, the record will show the property's title is in the name of a trustee. No one knows that John and Mary own the property. So, they have anonymity as the first layer of protection. They cannot be sued personally because they don't own the property.

Second, by transferring the beneficial interest of the land trust into an LLC, they are now protected from personal liability, with all the liability protection of the LLCs statutes. John and Mary are only members in the LLC. If the LLC, being the beneficiary of the trust, is named in the lawsuit, both John and Mary are still protected.

Members of an LLC are not responsible for claims or judgements against the company. When dealing with rental properties, or an active business, the potential liability associated with the business is a primary concern. This is the main reason to have the land trust's beneficial interest held in an LLC.

There is no better entity that will provide liability protection than the LLC. If something happens on the property, the LLC contains the liability from reaching anything else. If John and Mary are sued personally, for something, for example, let's use a car accident where someone got hurt, and they were found liable.

That judgment would not attach to their apartment building, because the property is no longer owed by them. It is owned by their land trust, and their LLC owns the beneficial interest in the land trust.

One Property, One Land Trust, One LLC

LLCs combined with the land trust are a great way to protect your investments. This will not only protect your assets but can minimize your tax burden. It's hard to predict a lawsuit, in fact, most people who encounter a lawsuit say, "but, I never saw it coming!"

I can't believe this is happening to me, I don't deserve this. Why me?

The best strategy to protect yourself from a lawsuit is be smart, and come up with an asset protection plan before getting sued. I always recommend that for highest liability protection, always use an LLC in conjunction with the land trust, making the LLC the beneficiary of the land trust. You now have privacy and liability protection for your real estate against a lawsuit claim, instead of just privacy alone.

You'd be surprised by how many investors wait until it's too late to protect their assets. Don't become one of them. They put multiple investment properties into one LLC, just to save money. You don't want to put several properties into one LLC.

If your LLC is sued and a judgment is awarded, the claim can possibly attach to everything that the LLC owns. Remember, an LLC keeps the legal liability inside the LLCs assets and doesn't let it attach to any personal assets that's outside of the LLC.

While you can't plan for every single contingency, you can put up several roadblocks and safety measures around your real estate assets to ensure you have maximum level of protection, should an unexpected event materialize.

The reason for safeguarding your real estate assets is simple, a failure to do so is like leaving your door open during the holidays and then wondering why a burglar stole everything inside. If you don't protect your assets before a lawsuit, your options are very limited to what can be done after a lawsuit has been filed against you.

Problems With Inside Liability

Having one LLC can protect from outside liability. Let's say, you have ten properties, offices, apartments, and houses in one LLC. You get sued personally for a car accident, medical malpractice, partnership or contract dispute. If the lawsuit is not related to the property held by the LLC, then having all your properties will work, because that liability is considered outside liability, because it is outside of the properties held by the LLC.

But, for maximum liability protection, it would be wise to have each property owned by a land trust and a separate LLC to hold each of the trust's beneficial interest. However, if you have a liability associated with a single property, and that property is mixed in with the other nine properties, it is considered inside liability. A lawsuit against the LLC, would subject all the properties to a judgment because they are owned by the single LLC. You could lose all of your properties by having them owned by a single LLC.

Again, to emphasize the point for maximum protection for your real estate, it should be one land trust and one LLC as the land trust's beneficial interest holder, for each separate property. If a lawsuit arises from the liability on a property, it would only involve that single property. Your other properties would not be attached, if a claim was awarded against the land trust as the owner of the property.

# CHAPTER 24 Fraudulent Transfers

Asset protection is always needed if you have assets. Protecting your assets from risk and liability is firmly established as a necessity in today's litigious society. But there comes a point in the law where financial transactions and legal proceedings are no longer allowed.

This happens when a lawsuit is filed against you. Laws in every state prohibit the transfer of property intended to hinder, delay, or defraud a creditor in order to avoid paying an imminent legal obligation. The law also prohibits transfers that leave you unable to meet your foreseeable obligations.

Although the law prevents you from creating an asset protection plan to evade current debts, it does allow for asset protection planning to avoid liability from future unanticipated creditors. As long as people have used real estate transactions, they have also attempted to conceal their ownership of property in order to defeat the claims of creditors.

To protect creditors from not being able to collect on their judgments, the courts have sought to invalidate transfers made with the intent to defraud creditors. Any transfer of property which is proved to be a "fraudulent conveyance" may be set aside by a court.

Under these circumstances, the transfers will be ignored, and the property will be subject to be seized by the judgment creditor. This law is currently embodied in the Federal Bankruptcy Code and the Uniform Fraudulent Transfer Act. Fraudulent transfers that fall into these categories can be reversed or set aside by four circumstances embroidered in the Federal Bankruptcy Code and the Uniform Fraudulent Transfer Act.

Judgment creditors use fraudulent transfer laws to reach assets transferred to a spouse, family member, friend, corporation, partnership, trust or any other third party. A creditor will be successful at reversing a transfer when they convince the court that the transfer was a last-ditch effort to defraud him. So, a fraudulent transfer challenge is often the true test of an asset protection plan.

To recover the creditor must prove: 1) there was a gift or transfer of property, 2) it was transferred less than fair market value,3) the transfer left the debtor insolvent.

This, of course simplifies the complex laws of fraudulent transfers. There are many differences of opinion between attorneys and courts as to what, constitutes a fraudulent transfer.

The fact that a creditor might, recover a fraudulently transferred asset does not necessarily mean that every creditor tries. Few fraudulent transfers are recovered because they are not discovered until the trial is over, and the value of the transferred asset may be too small to justify the creditor's time and expense to attempt recovery.

Moreover, there may be many creditors, and recovery by one creditor is not worthwhile to that creditor, when he must share the recovery with other creditors. Finally, the asset could be in a structure that will make it extremely costly and time-consuming to attempt recovery, such as an offshore structure.

# Chapter 25 Using a Wyoming LLC

Of all the states in the US, it's hard to beat Wyoming when it comes to its asset protection environment and anonymity. It's privacy laws and ease of operation makes it one of the best states to set up an LLC, if you want complete anonymity. It is inexpensive to set up and you get the maximum privacy and protection that's available in the US.

The state of Wyoming is not typically recognized as a true tax haven, yet it offers an ideal corporate environment for the formation of the LLC, for complete anonymity that keeps your name off all records. The LLC was first established in Wyoming and because of the strict privacy laws governing them, has become the preferred state to form an LLC for asset protection and anonymity.

The Wyoming LLC offers several benefits for business owners. To attain anonymity for all your LLCs, a Wyoming LLC is the first LLC to set up. It will hold title to the in-state LLCs. The primary attraction of the Wyoming LLC is that owners achieve privacy, fast and affordable incorporation with minimal reporting requirements that are not available in a public database.

**Your name does not appear on the formation documents and if asked for by anyone later, will not be disclosed. Your information does not go into any public database, to be researched. This is the main benefit of the Wyoming LLC, the complete anonymity of its members.**

The Wyoming LLC will be the base LLC and will be the manager member of all the other LLCs that hold properties. If someone is trying to find who owns the LLC in the state where the property is located, such as a disgruntled tenant, they will see that Wyoming LLC is the owner of the LLC. Then if the Wyoming LLC is searched for the ownership, they will find NOTHING.

**Equity Stripping with a Wyoming LLC using Anonymity**

IT'S EASY TO FIGURE out the equity in a property by the plaintiff's attorney. He simply goes online and on the Register of Deeds, he sees the dates of the mortgage notes. He then can determine approximately how much equity that you have in the property.

If he is suing for a greater amount than the insurance policy payout, the equity is what is going to pay the difference.

Let's pretend that you are the plaintiff's attorney, and you are going for the largest judgment possible to seek. You see the defendant's equity is $200K in the property. The insurance policy limits on the property are $300K. Why not go for the full $500K judgment? We have a property that we can get the equity out of, to satisfy the judgment, along with the insurance policy. It's inside liability, because the liability took place on the property.

How do we make the property look like it's not worth going after? Well in this situation we want to make this equity disappear. We do this by placing a mortgage lien on the property. We take our Wyoming LLC that is anonymous, because we don't want anyone to know that we have anything to do with this Wyoming LLC, and line of credit. We take this anonymous LLC that can't be traced back to anyone, because of its state statues.

We have the Wyoming LLC enter into a line of credit agreement between the Wyoming LLC and the property. The credit line would be at lease what the property equity is worth. In this example, it would be $200K. For this line of credit, the Wyoming LLC wants a deed of trust filed against the property. The purpose is that the credit line would encumber the property on title by the lien given to the Wyoming LLC.

When you searched the title, it would show a mortgage on the title from the Wyoming LLC. So, the property now has no equity. So that would discourage the plaintiff's attorney from a long court battle on attacking the property. He would go for the quick settlement with the insurance policy, and not the property. The whole strategy works because of the anonymity of the Wyoming LLC to prevent any information given about the members of the LLC.

**Wyoming's Protective LLC Charging Order**

ONE OF THE GREAT PROTECTION features of the LLC, is that creditors of LLC members are not allowed to satisfy personal obligations directly from LLC assets. The only remedy is a charging order. A charging order is a lien on distributions which may or may not be paid out as a member's distribution.

When a charging order is the exclusive remedy for creditors to reach assets of an LLC, the business is protected from the creditor's attempts to interfere with the business activities and force a payout.

However, the strength of the charging order is decided by each state. In a Wyoming LLC, the creditors cannot force the sale of the LLCs assets and must wait for distributions.

The same protection applies to single-member LLCs in Wyoming, where other states have limits for a single-member LLC, because the single-member LLC has no partner members to protect.

This is one of the best reasons for filing your LLC in Wyoming. The state's LLC statures that solely gives the creditor who wins a judgment, a charging order lien against the LLC's members distribution.

You have two options when setting up the LLC, as a "Member Managed" or "Manager Managed" LLC. A member managed LLC means that the members in the LLC have all the decision-making authority. So, they decide on what the LLC does, such as purchase or manage a property.

As a manager managed LLC, there is a manager that makes all the decisions of the LLC. The manager can be all the members, or members that hold a certain percentage of ownership of the LLC. It could also be one person appointed to be the manager of the LLC.

Registering as an LLC foreign entity in a non-Wyoming state, means you pay double annual fees and state taxes if applicable. This means that there would be an annual cost of LLC fees for both states and all additional costs of maintaining the registered agent for your Wyoming LLC. For an LLC to be valid and legal, it has to be registered in the state where the property is located.

If you are just starting out with just one property, the added expense may not be worth the cost of paying for each state's LLC, and a Wyoming LLC. To be clear, you have to form your LLC in the state where your property is located, since that is the state where your LLC is transacting business. When someone is searching the in-state LLC that holds the property, they would see that the LLC is owned by a Wyoming LLC.

If they searched the Wyoming LLC to see who owns it, they would not see any members listed, because the Wyoming LLC does not register who the members are. This is how anonymity is achieved using a Wyoming LLC.

# CHAPTER 26 An Offshore Nevis LLC

It's been known for many years in the asset protection world, that the most powerful and impenetrable way to protect assets is having an offshore trust located in another country. But because of the expense associated with setting up an offshore trust, these trusts were only established by ultra-wealthy individuals. They had the means and a reason for anonymity and asset protection. Well with modern technology, offshore trusts have now become popular with anyone that wants the ultimate asset protection for their assets.

Offshore asset protection involves transferring assets to a legal entity situated outside of the United States. People have heard of offshore trusts to hide their assets from debtors as long as they have been old enough to know what it meant. But there are other entities that can be set up to hold assets outside of the United States, along with trusts.

I know, I know, you've always thought that an offshore bank account is something shady, or even illegal. Or a way to be a tax cheat, and never pay taxes. These notions simply are not true. Offshore entities are a completely legal way to protect your assets. It is more expensive but may well be worth the price.

Setting up a foreign LLC is a bullet-proof asset protection strategy as it adds a layer between your assets and anyone filing a lawsuit to attain those assets. By using an offshore LLC rather than one in the US, you can enjoy additional protections simply not available at home. Because a US judgment is not recognized in Nevis.

A modern entity is the offshore limited liability company. It has the same benefits as a US LLC except greater. The Nevis LLC is now considered one of the best entities for holding your real estate assets in the name of the offshore LLC. Your real estate can be titled directly in the Nevis LLC, if it has no mortgage. If the real estate has a mortgage, I would first put the property into a land trust, with you being the beneficiary of the trust, and then assign your beneficial interest to the Nevis LLC.

The most popular offshore limited liability companies are in the Isle of Nevis, West

Indies. It's called a Nevis LLC and is a legal entity that one has established under the Nevis Limited Liability Company Ordinance. Nevis is an island located in the Caribbean Sea, located about 1200 miles from Miami.

**How an Offshore Nevis LLC Protects Your Assets**

A NEVIS LLC WORKS BETTER for holding real estate than an offshore trust, because it can hold assets outside of the US, and be managed by an individual or trust company, also situated outside of the US. There are many benefits to a Nevis LLC compared to the more well-known offshore trust. With a Nevis LLC you don't have the trust jurisdictions statutes that require the trustee be situated in their jurisdictions.

A Nevis LLC can be controlled and managed by anyone, anywhere in the world. You could serve as your own manager of the offshore LLC until such time that you had a serious creditor problem. If that ever happened, you could easily resign and appoint someone outside of the US to be a substitute or successor manager.

Most offshore trust jurisdictions require a significant amount of assets be in the jurisdiction where you set up the entity. The Nevis LLC Act however, does not require any assets to be held in Nevis. So, you could hold the real estate title, which is the beneficial interest in a land trust, in the Nevis LLC that would afford all LLC offshore benefits.

One of the best attributes of a Nevis LLC is the cost, and ease of forming and operating the Nevis LLC. The fees are substantially less than those required by an attorney to establish and operate an offshore trust. A Nevis LLC offers tremendous benefits of asset protection for real estate investors that need the greatest protection possible

that's not available in the US.

The Nevis LLC provides protection for both multi-members and single member companies. That is, it protects the members from losing their companies or the assets inside from personal lawsuits. The only remedy for a creditor is a charging order.

One must post a bond in Nevis courts before filing a lawsuit associated with a Nevis LLC. The bond has a minimum of $100,000 or any amount the court decides over this amount by the 2018 Legislature amendment. Establishing an LLC offshore can provide an additional layer of asset protection over US LLCs. You receive the most protection when you hold the assets in a foreign account in the LLC's name. This is because these assets are outside the reach of US courts. Plus, a Nevis LLC offers superior asset protection laws that exceed Delaware, Wyoming, and Nevada US LLCs statutes.

Nevis based LLCs are protected by a common law legal framework with several pieces of legislation through the country's "Limited Liability Company Ordinance" that created stringent financial privacy measures and confidentiality provisions ensuring maximum protection from public scrutiny.

A Nevis LLC has strong asset protection legislation that is often used as an alternative to a Trust, as a manager can be used and is similar to that of a trustee, and its members can be used similarly as a beneficiary. LLCs are also a very popular vehicle for joint venture arrangements that are arranged by various international jurisdictions as each venture can enjoy all the benefits and liability protection of the LLC, and each member is made only liable for taxation in their own country.

Placing the title of your real estate, or land trust beneficial interest, or for this example any assets into the Nevis LLC, doesn't mean that no creditor will ever be able to cash out on it. It does mean that it will be very expensive, and the creditor will have to go through a lot of extremely difficult steps. First, a Nevis LLC offers you protection against foreign judgments. Nevis does not automatically recognize a judgment from a foreign court, even one like the US.

To enforce a judgment in Nevis, a creditor must hire an attorney in Nevis. This is very expensive because contingency fee arrangements are not allowed in Nevis, so the plaintiff will have to pay their legal fees up front. In addition, all plaintiffs must file a

$100,000 bond to cover court costs, and the lawsuit must be filed against the LLC itself, not the individual member who owes the debt.

---

NEVIS ALSO OFFERS MUCH stricter protection against claims of fraudulent transfer than the US and most other countries. Nevis has an (two-year) statute of limitations for such claims, and the creditor is required to prove the fraudulent transfer beyond a reasonable doubt. Which in Nevis is a very high standard that is higher than most other countries.

Finally, punitive damages are not allowed in such cases.

**Nevis LLC Taxes**

TRANSFERRING ASSETS to a Nevis LLC does not trigger tax consequences associated with most other types of offshore companies This is because LLCs are generally tax-neutral where taxes flow through the company to the members. A Nevis LLC does not have any tax payment obligation. The obligation for any taxes that would otherwise be owned by the company bypasses the company itself and attaches directly to the members. Any other companies, as well as individuals and trusts, can be members of an LLC.

There are no limits for the number of members or the classes of members that an LLC may have. The important issue is that each member is responsible for his, her or its own pro-rata share of any overall tax obligation, if any, and that the LLC itself has no tax obligations. Also, a great thing about a Nevis LLC is that it is free from all forms of Nevisian taxation.

There are no Nevisian taxes on dividends, income, capital distribution, or wages whatsoever. Moreover, unlike many onshore jurisdictions, Nevis does not tax an LLC for accumulated, but undistributed earnings.

**Nevis Limited Liability Company Offers Maximum Privacy**

IF YOU HAVE A NEVIS LLC, you won't have to worry about your name ever being associated with the LLC. The government does not post the names of the members or managers of a Nevis LLC in the public records.

This provides for significant privacy. Nevis has strong privacy laws to prevent the registration, filing or disclosure of directors, shareholders of a Nevis Corporation or members or managers of a Nevis LLC. Since the beneficial owners and managers are not registered anywhere, a Nevis LLC provides complete anonymity and the best asset protection.

Therefore, there are not any initial or annual director filings in Nevis. Thus, the identity of the owners and managers are not attainable by any outside agency. Therefore, Nevis limited liability companies offer greater privacy than those of any country in the world.

All of the affairs of the LLC are private and cannot be disclosed except under extreme circumstances such as international terrorism.

**Nevis Asset Protection Features**

A NEVIS LLC ENABLES you to protect your assets and funds from government agencies, creditors, and lawsuits.

As an owner, you are not exposed to personal liability.

As an owner, you can participate in management without becoming personally liable for the debts.

A Nevis company is particularly advantageous for asset protection purposes since there are no shares that can be attached by a court of law.

Members are not liable for obligations of the company.

**Nevis LLC Charging Order**

THE NEVIS LEGISLATURE amended the Ordinance in 2015, which further increased the asset protection benefits of the LLC. It gives the same protection to a single-member LLC as multi-members ones, unlike the majority of US states. Nevis law establishes a charging order lien as the creditor's exclusive remedy. Thus, someone with a judgment against the owner of a Nevis LLC cannot take the LLC nor the assets inside.

For example, a US person or company attains a charging order against the Nevis LLC. The IRS requires a US person or business holding a charging order to pay taxes on that portion of a member's profits that the company earns. Moreover, they owe the taxes whether they receive the distributions or not. The right to receive the

distributions is the one responsible for the tax bill. It doesn't matter if the LLC paid out to the members or not, they still are responsible for the tax on the distributions to members. Charging order liens in Nevis expire after three years and are not renewable.

There is one benefit which Nevis has even over other jurisdictions which are friendly to offshore LLCs, and that is protection against charging orders. A creditor must obtain a charging order before they can recover any assets, and if they do, they will only be able to recover from distributions that the LLC makes to the members against whom the charging order was obtained.

If that isn't enough, the LLC has no obligations to pay the members whom the charging order is against, in addition, Nevis's charging orders expire after three years, and the creditor will have to pay taxes on the assets they recovered from the charging order, even if the creditor did not receive any distributions.

Nevis makes it nearly impossible for anyone to take your assets, with a charging order. This is one of the central reasons why offshore Nevis LLCs are so popular and offers some of the most powerful asset protection laws in the world.

# CHAPTER 27 The Limited Partnership

For many years, the family limited partnership or limited partnership was the cornerstone of asset protection planning. But in recent years, the limited liability company has become more prevalent in asset protection. But the limited partnership is still-popular, and is sometimes still the entity of choice, especially where the reduction of estate taxes is concerned.

A limited partnership has one or more general partners, and one or more limited partners. The general partner has the right to manage the partnership, but with that title, have unlimited personal liability for partnership debts. We improve this position for the general manager by setting up an LLC to be the general partner of the limited partnership, which effectively gives the general partner limited liability.

A general partner can also be both a general partner and a limited partner that holds an ownership interest in the limited partnership.

.

Limited partners on the other hand, have no managerial authority, and their personal liability is limited to their investment in the partnership. They are insulated from partnership debts in the same way corporate stockholders are from corporate debt. But corporate stockholders can lose their corporate shares to their personal creditors.

Partners in a limited partnership cannot lose their limited partnership interest to their personal creditors. This is the major difference between a limited partnership and a corporation.

In the limited partnership, general and limited partners contribute money, assets, or services for their partnership interest. The limited partnership is controlled by the general partner that has the authority to make all the decisions.

Since the general partner can incur liability for partnership debts, the general partner should be an LLC. So, creditors of the limited partnership can only pursue the assets of that LLC or corporation as the general partner.

A limited partner cannot manage or give orders or directives to the general partner but can provide advisory opinions. A limited partner's name should not be part of the partnership name, nor should a limited partner create the inference that the limited partner manages the business. Limited partners have the right to review partnership financial and legal records, name of other partners, and their contributions and profits.

General partners give the limited partners the tax information needed to complete their income tax returns. Unless otherwise stated in the partnership agreement, limited partners cannot be required to add more capital to the limited partnership. The limited partners voting rights are specified in the partnership agreement and the Uniform Limited Partnership Act.

Tax Treatment of Limited Partnership

Another major advantage of limited partnerships is partnership tax treatment. When compared to the corporation or sole proprietorship, the limited partnership has unequal tax advantages:

* Subject to certain restrictions, partners may distribute partnership income, gain, loss, or credit among the partners however they see fit.

**Seizure of Limited Partnership Assets**

THE LIMITED PARTNERSHIP offers a powerful tool that has been a cornerstone in asset protection for several reasons. With the limited partnership you can maintain complete control over your assets as the general manager and indirectly own the assets through ownership of a limited partnership interest.

Assets transferred to the limited partnership become fully protected and beyond the reach of any future creditor. A limited partnership in conjunction with an LLC are generally the most advantageous domestic entities for protecting assets. This is why they are the foundation for safeguarding assets within the U.S.

In a limited partnership, a creditor can only attempt to seize three types of assets,

a limited partnership interest, distributions payable to the limited partner, and the assets previously transferred to the limited partnership by the debtor.

**1. Limited Partnership Interest**

JUST LIKE THE CHARGING order in an LLC, a creditor of a limited or general partnership cannot seize the limited partnership interest. A judgment creditor of a limited partner can only have the court issue a charging order against the limited partnership interest. The charging order gives the creditor only the right to claim profit distributions payable to the limited partner. The charging order does not make the creditor a substitute partner.

Nor does it give the creditor any partnership rights, except the right to claim distributions payable to the debtor

The charging order's purpose is to protect the partners that are uninvolved in the debts of the partner who owes the debt, and from any interference in the affairs of the partnership. Unlike a corporation, where the debtor can force the sale of the debtor shareholder shares. This is a big distinction between a corporation and a limited partnership and makes the limited partnership highly useful in safeguarding wealth.

.

### 2. Seizure of Profits

IF THE CREDITOR'S RIGHT to claim distributed profits is the sole remedy, how practical is that remedy? Not very good if you consider its limitations. In most limited partnerships, the profits belong exclusively to the general partners, and all distributions are controlled by the general partners. The creditor cannot force a distribution.

The limited partnership can simply defer profit distributions to the debtor-partner until the charging order creditor loses patience and settles. The limited partner can also choose to receive loans, consulting fees or payment for other duties associated with profits. The debtor-partner can also divert profits to other interconnected entities that may transact business with limited partnership.

These funds would not be subject to the charging order because they are not a distribution of profits. Few creditors get a charging order, for the simple reason, the charging order creditor becomes liable to pay the taxes on partnership profits allocable to the debtor-partner, even when the creditor receives no payment or profit distributions from the partnership.

### 3. Recovering Assets in Limited Partnership

A THIRD POSSIBLE REMEDY is for the creditor to try to get the court to set aside assets and say they were fraudulently transferred to the limited partnership to avoid collection from judgment. This is a far more threatening possibility to the limited partnership than a charging order. So, to attain the assets in the limited partnership, the creditor must first rescind the prior transfer to the partnership as a fraudulent transfer.

Creditors have remedies when assets are fraudulently transferred to a limited partnership. For example, if you owe a creditor $100,000, and you transferred $70,000 cash into a limited partnership to avoid collection, the creditor could say this was a fraudulent transfer. This result, nevertheless, depends on how you have structured your limited partnership.

For instance, if you contribute $70,000 and your wife contributes the same amount, for a total $140,000 contribution, and you both own a 50% partnership interest, the court could say that is a fair contribution because you both own the same percentage of partnership. But if you said your partnership interest was disproportionately smaller, the court could rule that the percentage is fraudulent, and that some portion or all of the

$70,000 would be recoverable by the creditors. Even when the partnership consideration is fair, it does not guarantee that a court will not set aside such a transfer.

The law on this point varies between states and individual cases. You cannot assume that a transfer against a present creditor will not be set aside by the court. The limited partnership certainly provides greater protection than keeping assets titled in your name, and greater protection than a corporation has for its shareholders members.

From a debtor's position, the limited partnership shields partnership assets from all but the most determined creditor. A creditor must overcome numerous barriers before he can recover assets. As a practical matter, few creditors pursue a partnership interest or assets conveyed to the partnership unless the claim and the corresponding assets are exceptionally large.

First, you need a limited partnership agreement that spells out all the details of the partnership, and who will be the general partner, and the limited partners. You create the limited partnership by filing a certificate of limited partnership with the state who then issues a charter acknowledging the limited partnership's formal existence. Most state filings include the:

*Limited partnership name

*Address

*Name and address of general partners

*Name and address of registered agent

*Purpose of Limited Partnership

*Mandatory dissolution date

The certificate normally does not list the limited partners nor is the limited partnership agreement filed as a public record. Once your certificate of limited partnership has been filed and approved, go online to the IRS website and apply for an employer identification number (EIN). Complete and return Form SS-4.

Once the limited partnership obtains its taxpayer ID number, go to the bank and set up its own bank account. It's important to remember, that funds belonging to the limited partnership must be kept separate from your funds and other entities. Separate bank accounts and bookkeeping clearly show that this is a separate entity, if you ever needed to prove it.

# CHAPTER 28 Protect Your Assets Now

This asset protection information can prevent lawsuits from causing the destructive ramifications of losing your hard-earned assets to a lawsuit. No matter how much money you make in your lifetime, it's hard to justify the time and effort it takes to replace assets lost to a lawsuit, if it can be prevented. Life goes by too fast to start over again.

The first key in asset protection is action. Make a commitment to do so. As the saying goes, **"Dig Your Well Before You Get Thirsty."** You cannot impermeant these strategies while a lawsuit judgment is pending. You are strongly urged to follow these words: (DO IT NOW.) Your options are restricted if you are sued first.

If you have significant resources, you already know that this is the action you need to take now. If you do not have significant resources, this is the foundation upon which to build a strong financial future. Remember, it's your money, do what it takes to protect it.

Now you see why this famous quote by the richest man in history makes so much sense, especially in today's dangerous world, "Own Nothing, But Control Everything", (John D. Rockefeller.)

Writing this quote about Mr. Rockefeller make me think about a documentary, "The Men Who Built America" that I watched while I was in the hospital because of the Covid-19 virus.

A part of the documentary showed that John D. Rockefeller had scheduled a very important business meeting with Cornelius Vanderbilt about selling his large company. The meeting required Rockefeller to take a train up to see Vanderbilt in person.

Before catching the train, Rockefeller felt a compelling urge to visit his church to pray. Then, on the way to the train station from church, his carriage broke down. This caused him to miss the train and reschedule the most important meeting of his life. At the time, it was a great setback and a frustrating event for him.

A week later, he was startled to learn that the train he missed to go see Vanderbilt, had ended up derailing and falling off of a bridge in route. And everyone on the train had been killed. As you can imagine, this greatly impacted Rockefeller's life.

Decades later, Rockefeller reflected on this event and called it his "defining moment." It was that time in his life that made him realize he was on this earth for a reason. It was God that called him to the church, causing him to miss his train. And he was still alive because God had a bigger plan for him to carry out.

Writing the last chapter of this book, made me think of Mr. Rockefeller, and his defining moment in his life. I hope that somehow, and not in a self-severing egotistical way, that I have helped someone in their life be able to save their life savings and assets from a lawsuit claim. This is my way of giving back something, for the many blessings I have received in my lifetime. If I only help one person with this information, it was worth my time and effort in writing this book.

I know how hard it is in life to make money, and how heart-breaking it would be to lose it, because of an expected lawsuit. If you take only one thing from this book, it should be to get all your real estate assets out of your personal name, as soon as possible. Let's move that low-hanging fruit as high on the tree as possible, and not make it easy for a lawsuit to attach any assets.

It's important to realize, that a judgment can easily attach to anything that's in your name by just recording the judgment in the county where your property is located. A lawsuit comes when you least expect it, and as the wise owl says (who, who), it is referring to you. So. get that property out of your name. Your future self will thank you some day for your wisdom and action taken.

I have enclosed a land trust agreement as a sample at the end of this book, to help you. Please have your attorney make any needed changes to the land trust agreement to cover your personal circumstances and wishes. A recorded deed to your nominee trustee with the legal description will place your property into the land trust. Please remember, the land trust does not get recorded, only the deed to the nominee trustee.

Here's to you for educating yourself and taking the time to read this book. You now have the cornerstones to protect your assets, just as if you had hired an expensive asset protection attorney. Like the Klingons cloaking device in Star

Trek, you can now make your assets invisible, and protect them with an almost impenetrable shield.

"Thank you again for your readership, and I wish you success in your investments while traveling on life's spaceship, and boldly going to places that you're never gone before".

**Note: this sample land trust is for your reference only. You should NOT use it without consulting a knowledgeable attorney for your situation.**

AGREEMENT AND DECLARATION OF TRUST

«TRUSTNAME» LAND TRUST

THIS AGREEMENT AND DECLARATION OF TRUST Is made and entered into this «creationday» day of «Creationmonth», «creationyear», by and between «settlor» as Settlor, or Grantor (herein referred to as "Settlor" or Grantor,) whose address is

«Settloraddress», and «Trustee», whose address is «Trusteeaddress», (referred to herein as the "Trustee", which designation shall include all successor trustees,) for the benefit of «Beneficiary» as Beneficiaries, (referred to herein as the "Beneficiaries", whether one or more, which designation shall include all successors in interest of any Beneficiary),.

IT IS MUTUALLY AGREED AS FOLLOWS:

1. Trust Property. The Settlor or Grantor is about to convey or cause to be conveyed to the Trustee by deed, absolute in form, the property described in the attached Exhibit "A", which said property, herein referred to as "Trust Property", shall be held by the Trustee, in trust, for the following uses and purposes, under the terms of this Agreement.

1. Consideration. No consideration was paid by Trustee for such conveyance. The conveyance will be accepted and will be held by Trustee subject to all existing encumbrances, easements, restrictions or other clouds or claims against the title thereto, whether the same are of record or otherwise. The property will be held on the trusts, terms and conditions and for the purposes hereinafter set forth, until the whole of the trust estate is conveyed, free of this trust, as provided herein.

1. Beneficiaries. The persons named in the attached Exhibit "B" are the Beneficiaries of this Trust, and as such, shall be entitled to all of the earnings, avails and proceeds of the Trust Property according to their interests set opposite their respective names.

1. Interests. The interests of the Beneficiaries shall consist solely of the following rights respecting the Trust Property:

a.  The right to direct the Trustee to convey or otherwise deal with the title to the Trust Property as set out herein.

a.  The right to manage and control the Trust Property.

c. The right to receive the proceeds and avails from the rental, sale, mortgage, or other disposition of the Trust Property.

The foregoing rights shall be deemed to be personal property and may be assigned and otherwise transferred as such. No Beneficiary shall have any right, title or interest, as realty, in or to any real estate held in trust under his Agreement, or the right to require partition of such real estate, but shall have only the rights set out above, and the death of a Beneficiary shall not terminate this Trust or in any manner affect the powers of the Trustee.

1.  Powers of Trustee.

With the consent of the Beneficiary, the Trustee shall have authority to

issue notes or bonds and to secure the payment of the same by mortgaging the whole or any part of the Trust Property; to borrow money by creating notes signed by him in his capacity as Trustee; to invest such part of the capital and the profits earned by the capital and the proceeds of the sale of bonds and notes in such real estate, equities in real estate, and mortgages in real estate in the United States of America, as he may deem advisable.

a.  With the consent of the Beneficiary, the Trustee shall have the authority to hold the legal title to all of the Trust Property, and shall have the exclusive management and control of the property as if he were the absolute owner thereof, and the Trustee is hereby given full power to do all things and perform all acts which in his judgment are necessary and proper for the protection of the Trust Property and for the interest of the Beneficiaries in the property of the Trust, subject to the restrictions, terms, and conditions herein set forth.

a.  Without prejudice to the general powers conferred on the Trustee hereunder, it is hereby declared that the Trustee shall have the following powers, with the consent of the Beneficiaries:

(1) To purchase any real property for the Trust at such times

and on such terms as may seem advisable; to assume mortgages upon such property.

(2) To sell at public auction or private sale, to barter, to exchange, or otherwise dispose of, the whole of the Trust

Property or any part thereof, subject to such restrictions, for such consideration of whatever kind, and upon such

terms and conditions as may seem judicious; to secure payment upon any loan or loans of the Trust, by mortgage with or

without power of sale, and to include such provisions, terms, and conditions as may seem desirable.

(3) To rent or lease the whole or any part of the Trust Property for long or short terms, but not for terms exceeding the term

of the Trust then remaining.

(4) To repair, alter, tear down, add to, or erect any building or buildings upon land belonging to the Trust; to fill, grade, drain, improve, and otherwise develop any land belonging

to the Trust; to carry on, operate, or manage any building, apartment house, or hotel belonging to the Trust.

(5) To make, execute, acknowledge, and deliver all deeds, releases, mortgages, leases, contracts, agreements, instruments, and other obligations of whatsoever nature relating to the Trust Property, and generally to have full power to do all things and

perform all acts necessary to make the instruments proper and legal.

(6) To collect notes, obligations, dividends, and all other payments that may be due and payable to the Trust; to deposit the proceeds thereof, as well as any other moneys from whatsoever source they may

be derived, in any suitable bank or depository, and to draw the same from time to time for the purposes herein provided.

(7) To pay all lawful taxes and assessments and the necessary expenses of the Trust; to employ such officers, brokers, engineers, architects, carpenters, contractors, agents, counsel, and such other persons as may seem expedient, to designate their duties and fix their compensation; to fix a reasonable compensation for their own services to the Trust, as organizers thereof.

(8) To represent the Trust and the Beneficiaries in all suits and legal proceedings relating to the Trust Property in any court

of law of equity, or before any other bodies or tribunals; to begin suits and to prosecute them to final judgment or decree; to compromise claims or suits, and to submit the same to

arbitration when, in their judgment, such course is necessary or proper.

(9) To arrange, pay for and keep in force, in the name and for the benefit of the Trustee, such insurance as the

Trustee may deem advisable, in such amounts, and against such risks as deemed necessary by the Trustee.

1.  Duties of Trustee. It shall be the duty of the Trustee in addition to the other duties herein imposed upon them:

a.  To keep a careful and complete record of all the beneficial interests in the Trust Property with the name and residence of the person or persons owning such beneficial interest, and such other items as they may deem of importance or as may be required by the Beneficiaries.

a.  To keep careful and accurate books showing the receipts and disbursements of the Trust and also of the Trust Property, and such other items as they may deem of importance or as the Beneficiaries hereunder may require.

a.  To keep books of the Trust open to the inspection of the Beneficiaries at such reasonable times at the main office of the Trust as they may appoint.

a.  To furnish the Beneficiaries at special meetings at which the same shall be requested a careful, accurate, written report of their transactions as Trustees hereunder, of the financial standing of the Trust, and of

such other information concerning the affairs of the Trust as they shall request.

a. To sell the Trust Property and distribute the proceeds arising from such a

sale:

(1) If any property shall remain in trust under this Agreement for a

term which exceeds that allowed under applicable state law, the Trustee forthwith shall sell same at public sale after a reasonable public advertisement and reasonable notice to the Beneficiaries and, after deducting its reasonable fees and expenses, it shall divide the

proceeds of the sale among the Beneficiaries as their interests may then appear, without any direction or consent.

(2) TO TRANSFER, SET over, convey and deliver to all the then Beneficiaries of this Trust their respective undivided interests in any non-divisible

assets, or

(3) To transfer, set over and deliver all of the assets of the Trust to its Beneficiaries, in their respective proportionate shares, at any

time when the assets of the Trust consist solely of cash.

1. Compensation of Trustee. The Beneficiaries jointly and severally agree that the Trustee shall receive the sum of $ «trusteemonthlyfee» per month for his services as Trustee hereunder.

1. Liability of Trustee. The Trustee and his successor as Trustee shall not be required to give a bond, and each Trustee shall be liable only for his own acts and then only as a result of his own gross negligence or bad faith.

1. Removal of Trustee. The Beneficiaries shall have their power to remove a Trustee from his office or appoint a successor to succeed him.

1. Resignation and Successor.

a. Any Trustee may resign his office with thirty (30) days written notice to Beneficiaries and Beneficiaries shall proceed to elect a new Trustee to take the place of the Trustee who and sworn to by the Beneficiaries and containing an acceptance of the office, signed and acknowledged by the new Trustee, shall have been procured in a form which is acceptable for recording in the registries of deeds of all the counties in which properties held under this instrument are situated. If the Beneficiaries shall fail to elect a new Trustee within thirty (30) days after the resignation, then the Trustee may petition any appropriate court in this state to accept his resignation and appoint a new Trustee.

a. Any vacancy in the office of Trustee, whether arising from death or from any other cause not herein provided for, shall be filled within thirty (30) days from the date of the vacancy and the Beneficiaries shall proceed, to elect a new Trustee to fill the vacancy, and

immediately thereafter shall cause to be prepared a certificate of the election containing

and acceptance of the office, signed, sealed, and acknowledged by the new Trustee, which shall be in a form acceptable for recording in the registries of deeds of all the counties in which properties held under this instrument are situated.

    a. Whenever a new Trustee shall have been elected or appointed to the office of Trustee and shall have assumed the duties of office,

he shall succeed to the title of all the properties of the Trust and shall have all the powers and be subject to all the restrictions granted to or imposed upon the Trustee by this agreement, and every Trustee shall have the same powers, rights, and interests regarding the Trust Property, and shall be subject to the same restrictions and duties as the original Trustee, except as the same shall have been modified by amendment, as herein provided for.

    a. Notwithstanding any such resignation, the Trustee shall continue to have a lien on the Trust Property for all costs, expenses and attorney's fees incurred and for said Trustee's reasonable compensation.

1. Objects and Purposes of Trust. The objects and purposes of this Trust shall be to hold title to the Trust Property and to protect and conserve it until its sale or other disposition or liquidation. The Trustee shall not undertake any activity not strictly necessary to the attainment of the foregoing objects and purposes, nor shall the Trustee transact business within the meaning of applicable state law, or any other law, nor shall this Agreement be deemed to be, or create or evidence the existence of a corporation, de facto or de jure, or a Massachusetts Trust, or any other type of business trust, or an association in the nature of a corporation, or a co-partnership or joint venture by or between the Trustee and the Beneficiaries, or by or between the Beneficiaries.

1. Exculpation. The Trustee shall have no power to bind the Beneficiaries personally and, in every written contract he may enter into, reference shall be made to this declaration; and any person or

corporation contracting with the Trustee, as well as any beneficiary, shall look to the funds and the Trust Property for payment under such contract, or for the payment of any debt, mortgage, judgment, or decree, or for any money that may otherwise become due or payable, whether by reason of failure of the Trustee to perform the contract, or for any other reason, and neither the Trustee nor the Beneficiaries shall be liable personally therefor.

1. Dealings with Trustee No party dealing with the Trustee in relation to the Trust Property in any manner whatsoever shall have any obligation or privilege: to see that the terms of this Trust Agreement have been complied with; to inquire into the

authority of the Trustee, to inquire into the necessity or expediency of any act of the Trustee; or the terms of this Trust Agreement. Every deed, mortgage, lease or other instrument executed by the Trustee in relation to the Trust Property shall be conclusive evidence, in favor of any person claiming any right, title, or interest under the Trust, that at the time of its delivery the Trust created under this Agreement was in full force and effect; that instrument was executed in accordance with the terms and conditions of this Agreement, and, all its amendments, if any; and is binding upon all Beneficiaries under it; that the Trustee was duly authorized and empowered to execute and deliver every such instrument; if a conveyance has been made to a successor or successors in trust, that the successor or successors have been appointed properly and are vested fully with all the title, estate, rights, powers, duties and obligations of its, his or their predecessor in Trust.

1. Recording of Agreement. This Agreement shall not be placed on record in the county in which the Trust Property is situated, or elsewhere, but if it is so recorded, that recording shall not be considered as notice of the rights of any person under this Agreement derogatory to the title or powers of the Trustee.

1. Name of Trustee. The name of the Trustee shall not be used by the Beneficiaries connection with any in advertising or other publicity whatsoever without the written consent of the Trustee.

1. Income Tax Returns. The Trustee shall be obligated to file any income tax returns with respect to the Trust, as required by law, and the Beneficiaries individually shall report and pay their share of income taxes on the earnings and avails of the Trust Property or growing out of their interest under this Trust.

1. Assignment. The interest of a Beneficiary, or any part of that interest, may be transferred only by a written assignment, executed in duplicate and delivered to the Trustee. The Trustee shall note its acceptance on the original and duplicate original of the assignment,

retaining the original and delivering the duplicate original to the assignee as and for his or her evidence of ownership of a beneficial interest under this Agreement. No assignment of any interest under this Agreement, other than by operation of law, that is not so executed, delivered and accepted shall be valid without the written approval of all of the other Beneficiaries who possess the power of direction. No person who is vested with the power of direction, but who is not a Beneficiary under this Agreement, shall assign that power without the written consent of all the Beneficiaries.

1.  Individual Liability of Trustee. The Trustee shall not be required, in dealing with the Trust Property or in otherwise acting under this Agreement, to enter into any individual contract or other individual obligation whatsoever; nor to make itself individually liable to pay or incur the payment of any damages, attorney's fees, fines, and penalties, forfeitures, costs, charges or other sums of money whatsoever. The Trustee shall have no individual liability or obligation whatsoever arising from its ownership, as Trustee, of legal title to the Trust Property, or with respect to any act done or contract entered into or indebtedness incurred by it in dealing with the Trust Property or in otherwise acting under this Agreement, except only as far as the Trust Property and any trust funds in the actual possession of the Trustee shall be applicable to the payment and discharge of that liability or obligation.

1.  Reimbursement and Indemnification of Trustee. If the Trustee shall pay or incur any liability to pay any money on account of this Trust, or incur any liability to pay any money on account of being made a party to any litigation as a result of holding title to Trust Property or otherwise in connection with this Trust, whether because of breach of contract, injury to person or property, fines or penalties under any law, or otherwise, the Beneficiaries, jointly and severally agree that on demand they will pay to the Trustee, with interest at the rate of «interestrate» per annum, all such payments made or liabilities incurred by the Trustee, together with its expenses, including reasonable attorney's fees, and that they will indemnify and hold the Trustee harmless of and from any and all payments made or liabilities incurred by it for any reason whatsoever as a result of this Agreement; and all amounts so paid by the Trustee, as well as its compensation under this Agreement, shall constitute a lien on the Trust Property. The Trustee shall not be required to convey or otherwise deal with the Trust property as long as any money is due to the Trustee under this Agreement; nor shall the Trustee be required to advance or pay out any money on account of this Trust or to prosecute or defend any

legal proceedings involving this Trust or any property or interest under this Agreement unless it shall be furnished with sufficient funds or be indemnified to its satisfaction.

1. Entire Agreement. This Agreement contains the entire understanding between the parties and may be amended, revoked, or terminated only by written agreement signed by the Trustee and all of the Beneficiaries. This Agreement may be signed in counterparts, at different times and places.

1. Governing Law. This agreement, and all transactions contemplated hereby, shall be governed by, construed and enforced in accordance with the laws of the State of «State». The parties herein waive trial by jury and agree to submit to the personal jurisdiction and venue of a court of subject matter jurisdiction located in the County of

«County» and in the State of «State». If litigation results from or arises out of this Agreement performance thereof, the parties agree to reimburse the prevailing party's reasonable attorney's fees, court costs, and all other expenses, whether or not taxable by the court as costs, in addition to any other relief to which the prevailing party may be entitled. In such event, no action shall be entertained by said court or any court of competent jurisdiction if filed more than one year after the date the cause(s) of action actually accrued regardless of whether damages were otherwise as of said time calculable.

1. Binding Effect. The terms and conditions of this Agreement shall inure to the benefit of and be binding upon any successor trustee under It, as well as upon the executors, administrators, heirs, assigns and all other successors in interest of the Beneficiaries.

1. Trustee's Liability to Beneficiaries. The Trustee shall be liable to the Beneficiaries for the value of their respective beneficial interests only to the extent of the property held in Trust by him hereunder and the Beneficiaries shall enforce such liability only against the Trust Property and not against the Trustee personally.

1. Annual Statements. There shall be no annual meeting of the Beneficiaries, but the Trustee shall prepare an annual report of their receipts and disbursements for the fiscal year preceding, which fiscal year shall coincide with the calendar year, and a copy of the report shall be sent by mail to the Beneficiaries not later than February 28 of each year.

1. Termination. This trust may be terminated at any time by the Beneficiaries and with thirty (30) days written notice of termination delivered to the Trustee, the Trustee shall execute any and all documents necessary to vest fee simple marketable title to any and all Trust Property in Beneficiaries.

IN WITNESS WHEREOF, the parties hereto have executed this agreement as of the day and year first above written.

———————————————

SIGNED, SEALED AND DELIVERED IN THE PRESENCE

OF: (BENEFICIARIES) BENEFICIARIES

«Beneficiary»

ACKNOWLEDGMENT

STATE OF NORTH CAROLINA )

ss:

COUNTY OF ( ) )

Before me personally appeared ( ) to me well known and known to me to be the person described in and who executed the foregoing instrument, and acknowledged to and before me that ( ) executed said instrument for the purposes therein expressed.

WITNESS my hand and official seal in the State and County aforesaid, this ( ) day of ( ), 20 ( ).

NOTARY

SIGNED, SEALED AND DELIVERED TRUSTEE IN THE PRESENCE OF:

«Trustee»

ACKNOWLEDGMENT

STATE OF NORTH CAROLINA )

ss:

COUNTY OF ( ) )

Before me personally appeared ( ) to me well known and known to me to be the person described in and who executed the foregoing instrument, and acknowledged to and before me that ( )

executed said instrument for the purposes therein expressed.

WITNESS my hand and official seal in the State and County aforesaid, this (N) day of ( ) , 20 ( ) .

NOTARY

SIGNED, SEALED AND DELIVERED SETTLOR OR GRANTOR IN
THE PRESENCE OF: (SETTLOR)

«Settlor»

ACKNOWLEDGMENT

STATE OF NORTH CAROLINA )

ss:

COUNTY OF (NOTARY) )

Before me personally appeared ( ) to me well known and known to me to be the person described in and who executed the foregoing instrument, and acknowledged to and before me that ( ) executed said instrument for the purposes therein expressed.

WITNESS my hand and official seal in the State and County aforesaid, this ( ) of ( ), 20 ( ).

___________________________

NOTARY

# EXHIBIT "A" TRUST PROPERTY

**KNOWN BY STREET AND address as:**

# EXHIBIT "B"

## BENEFICIARIES AND THEIR INTERESTS

**Name and Address (BENEFICIARIES) Interest ( % )**

**NAME AND ADDRESS (BENEFICIARIES) Interest ( % )**

Dear Reader,

I am a real estate investor in Raleigh, North Carolina. If I can help you in any way or answer any questions, please contact me at

waynesbusinessmail@gmail.com

919-500-3377 cell

Thank you again for your readership and the purchase of this book.

To your success,

Wayne Richardson